D1179913

# Dust in Our Desks

## TERRITORY DAYS TO THE PRESENT IN ARIZONA SCHOOLS

Collected and Edited by
Alleen Pace Nilsen with Margaret Ferry and L. J. Evans
Arizona State University College of Education
Tempe, Arizona 85287

**On the cover:** West Prescott School photographed in March of 1878 by D.F. Mitchell and George Rothrock. *Arizona Historical Foundation photo.*
ASU College of Education Dean Robert Stout congratulating Margaret Ferry and L.J. Evans, the two ASU graduate students who helped collect the material for *Dust in Our Desks.*

Published through the support of ASU Centennial
Commission and College of Education
Dean Robert T. Stout



Printed in the United States of America under the
direction of the Arizona State University Media
Systems.

A special thanks to the late Jim Teofilo, who did the
initial design and publicity work on *Dust in Our Desks*.

ISBN C-9611932-2-0

# To G. Homer Durham, 1911-1985

President of Arizona State University, 1960-1969

# G. Homer Durham

Charles M. Woolf

G. Homer Durham was born February 11, 1911 in Parowan, Utah. He died January 10, 1985 in Salt Lake City, Utah, one day after he submitted the final copy of his article for this book.

Because of his contributions to education in the State of Arizona and at Arizona State University, where he was president from 1960-1969, this book is dedicated to his memory. The suggestion came from a group of school principals and superintendents meeting on the ASU campus the day following President Durham's death. It was a particularly appropriate suggestion because of his interest in history. At the time of his death he was Managing Director of the Historical Department of the Mormon Church.

President Durham's Bachelor's, Master's and Ph.D. Degrees from the University of Utah and the University of California at Los Angeles were in history and political science. When selected to be president of ASU, following the death of Grady Gammage in 1959, he was serving as Vice President for Academic Affairs at the University of Utah.

He arrived on campus in September of 1960 bringing with him a contagious enthusiasm for the academic future of ASU. It is often stated that he was ideally suited to be president during the 1960s when enrollments increased from 10,640 to over 25,000. Trained as a humanist and social scientist committed to the liberal arts tradition, he was an able speaker for academia and academic freedom. In one of his early reports, he described his goals for the new university as "the resurgence of the great quest for theory." He wanted a concern for fundamental theory and general principle to characterize the professional schools as well as the colleges of arts and sciences.

Those who served under President Durham were not only aware of his academic goals, but of his gregarious nature. He was people-oriented and had a commendable habit of touring the campus. Faculty members sitting in their offices would look up to see a smiling G. Homer Durham standing in their doorways. Teachers and students would be surprised to see him walk into a classroom, take a seat in a back row, and stay afterwards to discuss the subject matter with the instructor and remaining students. He and his wife, Eudora, rarely missed a university function whether it was a performance in Grady Gammage Auditorium, a reception on or off campus, or a basketball game in the old gymnasium. Students who had met him only once were surprised and pleased that he remembered their names. Faculty members were impressed, if not in awe, to observe him greet by name several hundred guests at receptions.

G. Homer Durham was a total university person with broad interests and an ability to converse on most topics, but he was a special lover of the arts. An accomplished musician and composer, it was not unusual for him to move to the piano and lead groups in singing. He had a great love for the state of Arizona and viewed the years he served as president of ASU as one of the pinnacle periods of his life. He will be remembered by those who worked with him and under him both for the leadership he brought to ASU and for his warmth as a human being.

---

*Charles M. Woolf, now Dean of the Graduate College, came to ASU in 1961.*

# Contents

# Preface

Alleen Pace Nilsen

The working title of this book was "A People's History of Arizona Schools," but we discarded that title when critics said its Bolshevik connotations were inappropriate for the uniquely American story we were telling. What we wanted to communicate was that we were not presenting a comprehensive history from one viewpoint, but instead a sampling from many individuals.

We announced plans for this book early last spring in a "Centennial Gazette" which went to historical societies, newspapers, and individuals. Approximately one-third of the stories were contributed as a result of this announcement. The others we went searching for. Collecting them was easier than getting them to fit in the allotted space. As our printing deadline drew near, more and more people heard about the project and offered new stories or suggested people to interview. If we could have begun where we ended, this would have been a better book, but perhaps it will inspire others to write their own histories.

Nominations for the 100 people listed on the Honor Rolls were solicited through a committee of educational leaders drawn together by Dean Robert T. Stout. The Honor Rolls are by no means complete, but we hope they will remind readers of the variety and the commitment that have characterized the best of Arizona educators. In the interest of space, people currently serving as full-time employees on the ASU College of Education faculty were excluded from consideration. Nor are people cited for current work as superintendents.

Gratitude for supporting this project goes to ASU's College of Education Dean Robert T. Stout and members of the Centennial Committee. Graduate College Dean Charles M. Woolf also deserves thanks for providing working time and other support. Pat Peterson was a model of patience in typing and retyping the manuscript. Dorris Moloso, Vera Walsh, Marian Hoyt and Jane Sanderson helped.

Individuals who contributed in such ways as supplying background information, encouraging others to write their stories, and loaning personal items and family photographs include Vera A. Barrett, John L. Bolles, Billie Cox, Don Jacobs, Rayna Larson, Beverly Merrill, Anne Oliver, Glenn and Maud Pace, Loretta Robson Pace, Virginia Reed, Susie S. Sato, Joe Spring, Paul L. Singer, Mary Thielemeir, Carl Wallen, and Betty Whetton. Ken Donelson deserves thanks for teaching me some things about editing. My husband, Don, and my children, Sean and Nicolette, also deserve thanks for patiently listening to each story.

Preparing *Dust in our Desks* has been an exciting project. I've learned that public education—like the weather—is something that everyone likes to talk about. However, people want and expect to do something about schools. It is almost impossible to read or listen to the news without being reminded that there are problems in education. I came away from editing this book convinced that, yes, Arizona schools have problems. But I also feel optimistic because the following pages put today's problems into perspective. Surely if our Arizona ancestors managed to solve their educational problems, then with some of the same grit, creative energy, and sacrifice, we too can succeed in meeting the challenges we face.

---

*Editor Alleen Pace Nilsen is Professor of Education and Assistant Dean of the Graduate College at ASU.*

# The 1800s: A Time of Dramatic Change

Long before Europeans set foot in what is now Arizona, children were undoubtedly being educated. Ample evidence from the remnants of buildings, irrigation systems, arts and crafts, and fortifications show that the Indian tribes who lived here were culturally advanced. Nevertheless continuous schooling in the modern sense of the word has a relatively short history.

In 1696, Father Kino established a mission at Tumacacori, and in 1700 he laid the foundation for the Mission of San Xavier del Bac near Tucson. During the next hundred years, other missions were established along the Colorado and Gila rivers, but they were intermittently raided and in the early 1800s were for the most part abandoned. When the United States acquired Arizona from Mexico in the mid 1800s, much of it was considered inhospitable desert or mountains, although several Indian tribes—Pima, Papago, Navajo, Maricopa, Hopi, and Apache—lived in the area. River valleys made good farmland, and grassy plains supported the cattle and horses of Mexican ranchers.

The American Civil War and the grand old mansions of southern plantations seem a world apart from the dry and rocky deserts of Arizona, yet in January of 1862 these two worlds came together when President Jefferson Davis signed an act admitting Arizona as a Territory of the Confederate States. Arizona was thought to have large quantities of gold which both the Confederacy and the Federal government needed. The United States Congress reacted to the prospect of losing this gold by passing its own bill to create the Territory of Arizona. Abraham Lincoln signed the bill on February 4, 1863.

In the 1860s, Arizona residents had problems they thought more urgent than educating their children. One was establishing law and order. Hostilities with the Apaches have been well publicized, but in addition outlaws from both Texas and California had for years been escaping the law by riding off into the wilds of Arizona. Such people did not bring families with them so they had no interest in building schools. Their presence also discouraged the kinds of settlers who would come with families. And much of the work that was available was temporary because it was connected with mining and freighting. As soon as the best ore was taken from a mine, everyone would literally pull up stakes and move on.

When the first Territorial legislators met in Prescott in the fall of 1864, Governor Goodwin asked for the establishment of public schooling saying that "self-government and universal education are inseparable." He urged the legislators to make a beginning, even though small, by setting aside a portion of the funds raised by taxation for the establishment of public schools.

The legislators took him at his word about making a "small" beginning and allotted $250.00 to the mission school at San Xavier del Bac. They also provided a matching fund arrangement of $250.00 for Prescott, La Paz, and Mojave, and $500 for Tucson. Most of the students who would go to these schools were Mexican, and one of the provisions stated for the Tucson school, was that English would be taught every day. Prescott may have used some of this money, but the only school known for sure to receive the allotted funds was the one at San Xavier.

The next two legislative sessions did little to encour-

Ash Fork School, 1893. *Arizona Historical Foundation photo.*

Tempe Normal, 1898.
*Arizona State University Archives photo.*

Little Adobe School in Tempe, 1885.
*Tempe Historical Museum photo.*

age public schooling. However private and church sponsored schools developed, although most of them were short-lived. W. H. Read, Edwin Darling, J. E. McCaffrey, S. C. Rogers, D. D. Chris, a Miss Blake, and a Mrs. Stephens were all mentioned in the Prescott newspaper, *The Weekly Miner*, as holding school during the 1860s. In Tucson, a Mr. Vincent opened a Catholic school for boys in 1866, and in 1870 the Sisters of St. Joseph opened a school for girls. Also on June 1, 1868 a treaty between the Navajo Indians and the U. S. Government established a reservation and guaranteed U.S. funds to provide education through the Bureau of Indian Affairs. In December of 1870, Presbyterian missionaries, Reverend and Mrs. Charles H. Cook, arrived at the Pima Indian Agency on the Gila River and established two village schools, one for Pima and one for Maricopa children.

The 1867 Legislative Assembly under Governor Richard Cunningham McCormick enacted a law giving towns the option of collecting taxes for schools. Tucson was the only town that took advantage of the new law. It set up a school in which Augustus Brichta, a well educated New Yorker who had come west in the gold rush of 1849, taught approximately 60 boys for six months.

School property taxes were made mandatory in the 1870s, but communities still had to scramble creatively for money. In cattle country, loose or stray calves were rounded up and put in the "school herd," contributions were taken at dances and parties, parents and townspeople donated labor, land, and materials, and an 1883 law specified that all money from fines, forefeitures, gambling licenses, and unclaimed estates would go to the Territorial School Fund.

Several of the controversies that divide educators today can be traced back to the late 1800s. These include who should select the textbooks and whether they must be the same statewide, whether women should be paid a salary equal to men's, how different certification requirements should be for high school and elementary teachers, and whether the State Superintendent of Public Instruction should be a political or a professional role, that is elected or appointed, and if appointed, by whom?

The biggest controversy of the period began in 1875 when the Legislative Assembly passed a bill providing $300 aid for the Sisters of St. Joseph school in Tucson. Out of 312 students enrolled in Tucson schools, 187 were attending Catholic schools. The parents of these children did not want to pay twice for their children's schooling, but the passage of the bill caused a quarrel between Catholics and non-Catholics. Its ripple effect went all through the state resulting in the forced resignation of the Chief Justice of the Territorial Supreme Court and the passage of several subsequent laws designed to keep public funds from being used to support religious education.

By 1883, the Legislature was accustomed to considering educational matters, and it established teacher training institutes, gave women the right to vote for school trustees, lowered to five the number of taxpayers required to create a school district, increased the number of required school subjects, and declared that ten percent of a district's funds (up to $200) could be used to establish school/community libraries.

The 1885 Legislature authorized the founding of a Territorial Normal School at Tempe and a University at Tucson. People in Tempe were so afraid that the 1887 Assembly would rescind the decision that they rushed to put up an impressive building and to be firmly established before the matter could be considered again. Classes in Tempe began on February 8, 1886. In Tucson, the people took their time because they had both more money and more confidence. Classes began there in 1891. The 1893 Assembly authorized the Northern Territorial Normal School and classes began at Flagstaff in 1899.

As the twentieth century drew closer, the legislature gave the Territorial Board of Education the responsibilities of establishing a uniform course of study, drawing up a list of books for school libraries, and controlling certification of teachers. Title XIX, passed in 1899, stated that all schools had to be taught in the English language. This law was the one later used by some districts as the reason for establishing separate schools for Spanish-speaking children.

The census of 1900 showed that Arizona had 428 public schools, 445 teachers, and 16,504 pupils. In addition, over 700 young people were attending church-sponsored schools. It is impossible in a book of this size to trace all the developments which within only thirty years contributed to such a dramatic change. However, the following pages provide glimpses from several angles.

# Anson P. K. Safford: The Father of Arizona Schools

Ernest J. Hopkins and Alfred Thomas, Jr.

Editor's Note: *The man commonly credited with starting Arizona's public education system is Anson P. K. Safford, who in April of 1869 was appointed by President Ulysses S. Grant to be Arizona's third territorial governor. Unlike many Territorial appointees, Safford was no stranger to the West. As a young man, he had emigrated from his childhood home in Illinois to California where he mined gold from 1850-1856. Then for the next three years he served in the California State Legislature where he was chairman of the Education Committee and helped draft some of California's first school legislation. In 1862, he moved to Nevada where he again was active in education concerns serving as one of three members of the State of Nevada School Board which wrote the first comprehensive education legislation for Nevada. Considering this experience, it is not surprising that when he was appointed to be Arizona's governor, he put the establishment of public schools as one of his top priorities. The following account of his success is excerpted from* The Arizona State University Story *by Ernest J. Hopkins and Alfred Thomas, Jr. (Southwest Publishing, 1960). It is reprinted by permission of Alfred Thomas, Jr.*

The Territorial legislature, elected in November, 1870, was to meet in January, 1871, and it was Safford's purpose to have it pass a Public School Act. He had made friends with Don Estevan Ochoa, outstanding Mexican leader, and, by a stroke of political genius, had converted him to the American public school idea; Ochoa would have naturally preferred the padres' parochial schools, but he was a legislator, and consented to introduce a public-school bill if Safford would prepare it. Safford had learned of some previous schools and school legislation in the Territory; the records were in his office, and it can be presumed that he studied them, in order to find out why these previous attempts had come to nothing by the time he arrived in Arizona . . . .

The 1871 Legislature approached, Safford having made his study, wrote his public-school bill. The measure Safford devised gave Arizona Territory the innovation that is most associated with his name—a Territorial System on top of the county and district systems—not dominating the latter, but aiding and coordinating them.

This Territorial system had highly original yet workable features. Its main purpose was to put steam behind a school-founding movement, the frontier's main need. Boldly shouldering this responsibility himself, Safford's bill made the Territorial Governor of Arizona the Superintendent of Public Instruction ex officio, providing him with $500 annual travel expenses, and commissioning him to make speeches, visit districts, and directly stimulate the establishment of schools. Safford felt himself the one man who could do the job, and the bill he wrote provided that he should do it himself as long as he was governor.

As to the county superintendents, he devised an extremely clever plan. As Governor, he already had the power of appointing, in each county, an official called the probate judge. These probate judges were among Arizona's ablest men; Charles Trumbull Hayden had held that office for Pima County, under Governor Goodwin. The Governor could appoint or remove them; they were responsible to him. Safford now hit on the logical idea of making the probate judges the county superintendents of schools ex officio, just as he was ex officio superintendent of the Territorial level.

A Territorial school tax was provided, also a Territorial Board of Education with power to standardize the textbooks, teacher-requirements, and other matters. Its members were the Territorial Treasurer and Secretary of State. The Governor himself was the third member and Chairman of this Board.

It all provided a Territorial school-starting and school-aiding machine. Only a local district could start or conduct a school, so that the localities were actually in charge. In practice, the people of a district would inaugurate a school movement, advised (if they wanted to be) by the probate judge as county superintendent; the judge would help get the district's application through the county board of supervisors; the Territorial officials would set the standards. There would be taxes for school purposes on all three levels—district, county, and state.

Safford's own curtly worded report sent later to the Federal Bureau of Education at Washington, tells what happened to that bill:

> I prepared a school bill and presented it to the Legislators as soon as they were assembled. Scarcely a member looked on it with favor. They argued that the Apaches were overruning the country, that through robbery and murder the people were in poverty and distress, that repeated attempts had been made to organize schools and that failure had always ensued.
>
> To these objections I replied that the American people could and would ultimately subdue the Apaches; that unless we educated the rising generations we should raise up a generation no more capable of self-goverment than the Apaches themselves; and that failure to establish schools had been due to imperfect statutes.
>
> Finally, on the last day of the session, they passed the bill, after striking out nearly all the revenue which had been provided.
>
> The measure was the best that could be secured and had to be accepted as it was.

A bitter victory! Safford's public-school system was established, on paper, but the legislative hatchet-men had cut out the funds. On February 17, 1871, "The Little Governor" signed the emasculated version of his two-year dream. He might have felt bitter—but he didn't . . . .

The five-mill Territorial tax with $500 for travel expenses had somehow escaped the legislative axe—and a local school district, if its people decided to form one, still had power to tax itself.

History says that without loss of a day this 140-pound bundle of courage threw bacon, coffee, and blankets into his buckboard, hitched up his two mules, and set out on the desert roads, alone to visit the widely scattered settlements of Arizona Territory, at the height of the Apache wars.

He was going over the heads of the legislators, to talk to the people directly . . . .

Arizona roads, apart from the deep-rutted "through" routes, were nil in 1871. The usual way of getting to a settlement was to head in that general direction, steer by the shape of the country or by the stars, and take the open desert.

Safford was to do this for the next six years. Historians, who have marvelled at his one- man public-education crusade, regard him as a sort of Lone Ranger of Education. They agree that sooner or later "The Little Governor" visited every settlement in 'Arizona's 113,000 square miles, performing his other gubernatorial duties between trips . . . .

Safford's own account of his crusade was a model of understatement. As he later reported it to the Bureau of Education:

> As soon as the Legislature (of 1871) adjourned, every part of the State was visited, and appeals to aid in establishing schools under the law . . . were everywhere made. A desire for schools soon began to appear among the people . . . . In the course of the following year, several schools were in operation . . . .

Safford had started his crusade late in February. All through that year of 1871, not a school resulted from his efforts. However, [his] earnestness and vigor were having an effect. Toward the end of the year there were preliminary rumbles in various communities; then, in the early months of 1872, after he had been a year on the road, a flashpoint was reached. Seven public schools came into existence almost simultaneously and, later in 1872, an eighth.

Typical of what was going on was a preliminary development at the Capital, early in November, 1871. The Pima County Supervisors appointed a board of trustees consisting of W. F. Scott, Samuel Hughes, and W. C. Davis; on Nobember 15, they rented a 20 foot by 40 foot adobe for $16 a month for nine months and put up $300 for school furnishings. On March 4,

1872, this school opened, under a capable young teacher, John Spring.

When the first Phoenix school was opened is in doubt; some give January 1, 1872, as the date, others as late as September 2. Both dates may well be correct, one for the preliminaries, the other for the opening. This school had its quarters in the Maricopa county court house on First Avenue south of Washington Street; later it had a little building of its own . . . .

The former S. C. Rogers school at Prescott was reopened February 1, 1872, under the local pastor, the Reverend Gilmore. Funds were short— the school closed down April 9, reopened May 1, then struggled along until June 29 with 31 pupils. The next year it got permanently on its feet; but it's good to remember that none of those early-day public schools was easily born.

Two weeks after the Prescott opening, Arizona City (Yuma) started its first school, in an abandoned jail. The date was February 15, 1872; the teacher was Miss Clara A. D. Skinner, the first woman teacher in Arizona. This "calaboose academy" soon required a second teacher and Miss Francis V. Bishop became Miss Skinner's assistant. The funds lasted until June . . . .

When the Seventh Legislature assembled in 1873, it was a very different story from that of 1871. The legislators had "heard from home." They touched up the Safford-Ochoa Act at Safford's request, restored the deleted county school tax and made it compulsory, increased the Territorial tax from 10 cents to 25, and tackled the knotty problem—not yet fully solved today—of the apportionment of school funds. What they did was interesting. The average daily attendance basis had been found unsuited to an area where flash floods, Indians, or other frontier contingencies might interrupt school attendance at any time. The enrollment basis favored the larger and older schools financially. So they fell back upon the population of school age residing in each county, to be determined by an annual school census—a most logical plan, since it showed the number of young people to be educated. Although later legislatures were to refine and revise the original Safford Act of 1871 several times, Stephen B. Weeks of the Federal Bureau of Education has called all later laws "only the Act of 1871 writ large." Today's Arizona school set-up can be traced directly back to the Safford public school Act of 1871 without a break.

The year 1873 was a turning point for Arizona in many respects. General [George] Crook, sent into Arizona at Safford's insistence, was getting the Apaches under control . . . . Mining, stockraising, and transportation all were reviving, irrigation along the Salt River had started and farming was taking hold; new settlers were pouring in at a rate that, from 1870 to 1880, multiplied Arizona's non-Indian population by four . . . .

"The Little Governor" kept up his educational trips until the end of his Governorship in 1877. When Safford retired from the Governorship, Arizona had 28 public schools with 3,089 pupils and 37 teachers—a flourishing start.

Tempe school children 1885.
*Tempe Historical Museum photo.*

---

*Alfred Thomas, Jr. served as University Archivist at ASU until his retirement in 1984.*

# Coming to Ehrenburg in 1872

Mary Elizabeth Post

After spending about two months in the vicinity of San Diego, with the family of an uncle, I was at the Horton House all ready to return to San Francisco by the next steamer when the call came from Ehrenberg, 800 miles away, for a teacher. The proprietor of the stage line from Yuma to Mesilla, N.M., called upon me at once to see if I would accept the position, or whether he must look farther. He said I must decide at once, as the next stage left Wednesday evening, (this was Monday), and they wanted to send a teacher by that time if possible. After obtaining all the information available, I finally changed my plan and prepared for a stage ride of two days and nights instead of an ocean trip of three or four days.

I was told that the weather was very warm in Arizona, so I should take only my very thinnest clothing and since only thirty pounds of baggage was allowed, I should take only the most necessary things. The porter at the Horton House (then quite the best hotel in the Southwest), at the suggestion of the stage proprietor, bought for me a little trunk, such as he had bought for other ladies who had made the trip, and I was told that if it was a little over the stipulated weight, no excess baggage would be charged.

I bought a broad brimmed hat to protect myself as much as possible from the sun, which already was becoming quite ardent, packed that little trunk and left on the evening of the eleventh of April 1872 on that long stage ride, my first experience of the kind. The parting words from the stage proprietor, who had come down with his wife to see me off were revelations that were a little disquieting. He told me not to be frightened if a sand storm should come up and the driver should lose his way, that he would turn the team around so as not to face the wind, and wait until it was over, then find the road again. So they had real sand storms, such as I had read about in the Sahara desert!

Then he said when I reached Yuma, where I might have to wait several days for a steamer to go up the river, not to go to a hotel, as there were so few ladies traveling in Arizona that the amount of attention they attracted made it quite unpleasant. I should have the stage driver take me to the house where the two Yuma teachers were and stay with them while waiting.

The vehicle in which the trip was made was not a Concord stage, such as was afterwards put upon the line, but what was known in common parlance as a "mud-wagon." It had two seats, and could carry three persons besides the driver, was covered with canvas as a protection against the sun, with curtains on the sides which could be raised or lowered at pleasure . . . .

It was hoped by my friends that I would be the only passenger, as that would give me some room to recline for rest, but when we were ready to start, there was an Indian agent for the Sacaton Agency with considerable excess baggage, and a merchant from Florence returning from San Francisco, where he had been to replenish his stock of goods, so there was nothing to do but sit erect in the stage for forty-eight hours, the only respite being the short stops made three times each day for meals.

The food supplies, as can be easily understood, were entirely of such things as will bear transportation well, and could be kept for some time. But as we came in sight of the last station before going down upon the desert, the gentlemen of the party said that we were to have "Arizona strawberries" for dinner. Although wondering a little at the statement, I asked no questions, and when the dinner was served I made my first acquaintance with the pink beans which still form such a staple article of diet, at least in the isolated regions of Arizona.

About four o'clock of the second morning of our journey, the gentlemen noticed that the driver seemed to be going this way and that, quite uncertain of his way, so they asked him if he had lost the road. He acknowledged that he had, but said that he should soon find it, that the station was just over there, pointing in an easterly direction.

They said we will not go a step farther until we know just where we are going, so they made him stop, and they gathered up material for a beautiful bonfire. We sat on the sand and enjoyed its light and warmth until morning dawned, when we could see the station in just about the direction that the driver had pointed. We soon found the road and went on our way rejoicing.

I really made the trip with far less fatigue than I had anticipated. I found that by leaning against the canvas cover I could go to sleep at almost any time, so I did not lose much sleep and reached Yuma in better condition than I had thought possible, where I received a warm welcome from the teachers and County Superintendent, to whom I had brought letters of introduction. The ten days spent in Yuma, waiting for the steamer passed very pleasantly, but during that time I never stepped into the street alone, not that it was really dangerous to do so, but the amount of attention attracted made it more comfortable to have a companion.

The steamer trip was quite as novel an experience as the stage ride had been. The only steamers I had ever seen were those of Lake Champlain, and of the Hudson and Mississippi Rivers, with their crowd of passengers, and when the lady who had accompanied me on board finally left me there on that afterdeck alone, the only lady on board, I would gladly have retired into one of the two little state rooms, there, to escape that staring crowd on the bank, if I had only known which was mine.

Turning my back to the crowd I was trying to be comfortable in spite of my surroundings, when the captain with a bottle of whisky in one hand and glasses in the other came back to the "olla" which was on this deck, and in company with a friend frankly drank in my presence which added much to my discomfort.

The absence of guards on the edge of the decks, gave one a very uncomfortable feeling of insecurity, and sudden gusts of wind took things overboard. I lost my hat in this way, before I had learned to guard against the danger, and as it was the only one I had with me, I was wondering how I could go ashore at my destination, but I was reassured by the County Superintendent, a passenger, who told me it was not the universal custom there to wear hats, that a veil would answer every purpose.

That evening one of the leading merchants of the place called upon me and presented me with a hat from his store, the like of which I have never seen, before, or since, but in consideration of the kindly feeling which prompted the gift I wore it during the five months I remained in Ehrenberg. I ripped off the multiplicity of flowers and other trimmings it bore, bound the edge securely and put a plain band around it, and made of it quite a respectable utility hat.

Ehrenberg was a thriving village of about five hundred inhabitants doing a business quite out of proportion to its population. The freight both civil and military for many interior places passed through it, and I was surprised at the size and the good quality of the stock of goods carried by the merchants. A place which had formerly been occupied as a saloon was prepared for a school room.

It was an adobe building, with an earth floor, very thick walls, which were simply rows of arches with columns between, and a roof resting upon them. The arches were closed at night by heavy wooden doors, opening inward. There were no windows, but when the doors of all the arches were opened in the morning it was practically an out-of-door school; at least we had plenty of light and air.

Tables and benches were placed here for teachers and pupils and the school work began under great difficulties, for the teacher knew not a word of Spanish and the children not a word of English. Occasionally a former patron of the place, who had been away from town for some time, wandered in, but when he found it occupied by a teacher surrounded by her children he backed out with profuse apologies. Five months of this work brought teacher and children much nearer together; the teacher had learned some Spanish, the children some English and in many other ways had approached each other.

In October, 1872, (the first school had begun in February of the same year), I took charge of the Yuma school. They had had a few months already, but there was by no means the interest in school matters that the public spirited citizens of Yuma wished to see.

The building here was the one previously occupied as a jail, and the walls were still ornamented with the scrawls, covered though not hidden by whitewash, with which the former occupants had whiled away their time. The building on the opposite side of the street from the school house was now leased for the court house and jail, and here during the first school year in Yuma occured a very gruesome incident.

A very brutal murder had been committed in Yuma in October, 1872, and the murderer had been found, tried, convicted, and sentenced to be hung a certain Friday in May, 1873. The day before this they worked all day, erecting a gallows in the yard outside the jail, just across the street from my school-room, in plain sight of all my children, and where every sound of the hammer could be heard.

When the hour of closing came on Thursday night, I informed the children that there would be no school the next day, although I had received no notification to this effect, and on my way home I stopped to notify the trustees also, as they had failed to notify me. This was the first legal execution that took place in Arizona.

It will be impossible in a short magazine article, to more than hint at some of the pioneer work in the Yuma schools, and the results to which it has led. The public spirited men of Yuma were determined to make the schools popular at all costs, and I soon found that my work lay quite as much outside the school room as in. As the great majority, in fact, nearly all of my pupils were of Spanish extraction, it became necessary for me to learn that language in order to get in touch with the mothers.

I applied myself with all diligence to the task, which was comparatively easy, as I had been teaching French and Latin for years. The citizens were always ready to raise money for entertainments for the children, so we had Christmas tree and May Day picnics in which the whole town joined with the greatest interest. As the beauty of a children's fete depends so largely on the costumes of the children, I found that here was a place where I could be of real service outside the school-room, which would help indirectly to further my work.

This was before cut paper patterns of garments were as popular and cheap as they are now, but the *Delineator* was already an acknowledged fashion magazine. They offered a package of fifteen dollars worth of patterns for ten dollars if ordered at one time. So I ordered a pattern that would fit each little girl in my school. When they came, I went around from house to house and cut the dresses and showed the mothers how to put them together, and when Christmas came, I doubt if there was a better dressed company of children in all the land.

When May Day came, we had our picnic either up or down the river at a place previously prepared, where music, dancing, games of all kinds for the children, the most delicious lunches available, and every little girl in a pretty white dress, helped to make a memorable day in the lives of all the participants, old and young, for the mothers enjoyed the day as much as the children.

The day is now past when such work is necessary in the same degree. Instead of trying to make the schools popular, we are striving to make provision for those who come to us, excluding carefully all those who are under age, as we lack the room for those who are of school age. We now have a well organized High School, in addition to our eight grades, 21 teachers instead of one, and prospects for rapid increase.

---

*Mary Elizabeth Post wrote these memories for the* Arizona Magazine, *Vol. 2:5 (February, 1912) under the title "Experiences of a Pioneer Teacher." 1912 was the year that she retired at age 70 and was the inspiration for Arizona's first teacher retirement appropriation.*

# Honor Roll: the 1800s

| | |
|---|---|
| **John Samuel Armstrong** | In 1883, school teacher Armstrong moved to Tempe and shortly thereafter was elected to the territorial legislature. In January of 1885, he convinced the group to approve the founding of the Normal School in Tempe. |
| **Bradford Farmer** | A Latin scholar educated in upstate New York, Farmer came to Prescott to teach and in 1885 was hired to be the first principal and the entire faculty of the Normal School. |
| **Charles Trumbull Hayden** | Before he was 23 years old, Hayden had taught school in Connecticut, Indiana, and St. Louis. In 1848 he used his savings to move west as a freighter eventually settling in what is now Tempe where he was influential in founding the Normal School. |
| **James McNaughton** | McNaughton was the first president of the Normal School to have a Ph.D. Under his presidency from 1895 to 1899, Old Main was completed, student government was founded, and the Normal School curriculum was changed to a three-year course with high school students being excluded. |
| **Estevan Ochoa** | Ochoa, a successful and well educated southern Arizona businessman, was the legislator who in 1871 worked with Governor Safford to draw up and introduce the bill establishing Arizona's public school system. |
| **Hugh Patton** | Patton, a Pima educated at out-of-state boarding schools, was the first teacher hired for the Phoenix Indian School. He taught in the early 1890s, and then returned to the reservation to run a trading post. |
| **S. C. Rogers** | Prescott was the first community in the territory to have a public school. S. C. Rogers and D. D. Chris were the teachers. In 1870, Rogers persuasively wrote about the problems he faced and made recommendations which were incorporated into the Ochoa-Safford school law of 1871. |
| **Anson P. K. Safford** | In 1869, when Ulysses S. Grant appointed Safford to be the third territorial governor of Arizona, there was not a single public school. Eight years later, mostly thanks to Governor Safford's efforts, Arizona had 28 schools, 3,089 students, and 37 teachers. |
| **E. L. Storment** | After succeeding in the frontier community of Agua Caliente, this young teacher was offered the assistant principalship of the Normal School when he was only 25-years-old. He became principal in 1892 and founded both the alumni association and the training school. |
| **George and Martha Wilson** | In 1885, the Wilsons agreed to sell five acres of pastureland to be the site of the Normal School. However, the legislators specified a minimum of 20 acres, and so without asking for additional money, the Wilsons deeded their whole 20-acre pasture to the new school. |

# Assimilationist Education at Phoenix Indian School

Robert A. Trennert

The federal commitment to educating Indian children dates back well over a century and has always been wrapped in controversy. Until recently this commitment focused solely on preparing native youngsters for assimilation into American society. Indeed, during the last decades of the nineteenth century, when the emphasis on assimilation reached its peak, government schools exerted every effort to blot out traditional Indian cultures and replace them with the values of middle-class Anglo-American life. The emotional pressure placed on Indian students was substantial, and the actions of ethnocentric administrators could create bitter resentments. Such was the case at Phoenix Indian School, which by 1899 was the largest BIA (Bureau of Indian Affairs) institution in Arizona. To understand the conditions which brought some of the school's pupils to draw up a letter expressing a feeling of mistreatment, it is first necessary to know something of the historical development of Indian education in Arizona.

Immediately following the Civil War the federal government turned its attention to the assimilation of the native population. Merging tribal members into mainstream society was believed by many experts to be the most effective and humane method of solving the "Indian problem." A practical way of accomplishing this goal seemed to be through education—taking native children from their homes and placing them in schools that taught English and stressed traditional American values. Although day schools were established on some Arizona reservations as early as 1872, they never met with much success. The Indian Bureau preferred off-reservation boarding schools. Inspiration for such schools came from the Carlisle Indian School in Pennsylvania, where Captain Richard Henry Pratt had established an institution devoted to Indian assimilation. Pratt's basic philosophy centered on separating the Indians from their traditional environment, teaching them the nobility of manual labor, and having them associate with white society. In this way, he predicted, the Indian would become "civilized" and find a place in the modern world.

Placing an off-reservation boarding school in central Arizona seemed especially appropriate during the mid-1880s. The Pima and Maricopa Indians had been friendly to Americans and were in need of educational help. Located on reservations near Phoenix, their agents had long recommended the establishment of a boarding school to remove children from the influence of their untutored parents. Educators of that era generally maintained that students who remained close to home could never be weaned of "their old filthy ways." As a consequence, in 1891, the federal government opened a major nonreservation school in Phoenix, patterned after Carlisle and intended primarily for the benefit of the local tribes.

After spending a year at a makeshift building in downtown Phoenix, the school moved to its present location on Indian School Road, then about three miles north of town. The training focused on total assimilation. Most of the pupils were "raw recruits," children directly off the reservation who had little or no prior contact with the white man's way. Coming from traditional Indian lifestyles where learning was informal, youngsters were often unprepared for a structured school experience. Students first went through a process called "de-Indianization" where they were given baths, new clothes, and hair cuts. Then they were subjected to a strict routine of discipline. Boys and girls were organized into military-style companies, dressed in uniforms, and forced to obey orders. English was the only language permitted, and corporal punishment regularly followed a violation of rules. Half of the day was spent in the classroom and the remainder devoted to work training. Young men learned "practical skills" such as blacksmithing, carpentry, and farming. Girls spent their days acquiring such domestic skills as cooking, sewing, and washing. Church services on Sunday were mandatory, and all social contact between the sexes was closely supervised.

Despite the oppressive structure of this system, local tribes came to appreciate the school. They regarded it as their school, and since it was close to the reservations, parents were able to visit their children. In addition, the government provided pupils with good care—plenty of food, medical treatment, and warm clothing. Some tribal leaders even acknowledged that the future of their people rested in education. Unfortunately, school administrators were reluctant to let the children develop at a reasonable pace. The government wanted immediate success; something that was impossible. Students found school difficult, had to spend considerable time learning English, and were unable to participate in advanced classes. As a result, most pupils, regardless of age, struggled at levels equivalent to kindergarten. Schoolmasters were keenly aware of this fact. They felt the school could not be a successful part of the assimilation program unless it attracted more advanced students.

This was the situation when Samuel McCowan increased enrollment to 700, constructed a modern campus, and graduated the first class (at the eighth grade level). He was a dedicated man who put up with no foolishness. As he stated in 1898, "We pride ourselves on being a working school. No child is permitted to work as he pleases. 'putting in time' is not sufficient. The child is taught how to do a thing, when to do it, and to do it whether he wants to or not."

Ironically, the headmaster was unimpressed with local Indian children. He believed the Pimas and Papagos were so "primitive" that the school could never make progress as long as its student body was drawn primarily from nearby tribes. Therefore, one of his first measures to improve the school involved bringing in Indian students from other areas. McCowan recruited pupils from the Navajo, Hopi, and Apache reservations, and even went to California and New Mexico for new students. Most of the children he imported had some prior schooling and were capable of doing advanced work. Although they made the school appear more successful, the "foreign" students were not well received by local Indians. Students from the nearby reservations were quick to notice an air of discrimination, and in 1899 they sent a petition to the Commissioner of Indian Affairs protesting the actions of superintendent McCowan. In the document printed below (which was written for them by a white friend) the Pima, Maricopa, and Papago students show how much they valued the school, and how they were treated by a heavy- handed schoolmaster. In all fairness, it should be noted that McCowan departed in 1902 and the local tribes eventually came to accept the mixture of tribes at Phoenix. Still, this petition illustrates some of the harsh realities of assimilationist education in Arizona during the nineteenth century. The Indian Bureau never responded to the student complaint.

April 13, 1899

WHEREAS

The Indians of the Pima, Papago and Maricopa tribes have a complaint to lay against S. M. McCowan, Superintendent of the U.S. Indian School at Phoenix, Arizona. They humbly petition your consideration of the same.

Since July 1897 when said S. M. McCowan was appointed to the position he now occupies, he has made himself odious to Indians of said three tribes both in regard to administration and demeanor.

Moreover in consequence of the wide-spread aversion to said McCowan among the Indians of said three tribes, said McCowan has experienced great difficulty in finding children to occupy the school, and as a result has sought to do so by obtaining them from various other tribes, resident in California and elsewhere.

There are moreover many of these so-called Indians, who are it is believed, pure Mexicans, and others who show absolutely no trace of Indian blood, being to all appearance white children.

We, the Pima, Papago, and Maricopa Indians resident at the U.S. Indian School of Phoenix, Arizona, aforesaid, object to such a course of action, seeing that this school, having been established in the native country of these three tribes was designed more especially for their education and civilization. We are convinced moreover that it is not the intention of the Government to allow such a policy to be persisted in, regarding it a gross injustice, for the time is not far distant when if Mr. McCowan's administration continues the school will be filled with Indians from other tribes, no place being found for the native Indians of this country to their present disadvantage and permanent detriment.

We would prefer that the policy of Mr. Craiger, ex-superintendent of the U.S. Indian School at Albuquerque, N.M. be employed in relation to applicants for admission to this school. This gentlemen is well known to have always caused the most searching investigation to be made before admitting a child to the school. We strongly object to a policy which favors the admission of all classes of children on application without due discrimination.

Moreover from what has been seen and heard we believe said S. M. McCowan has no sympathy for the Indians and is consequently unfit to fill the position he now occupies.

On the morning of March 30th ult° when Ramon Johnson, a Papago boy at the date resident in this school, was irrigating, said McCowan gave him instructions, which speaking but little English he failed to understand, said McCowan immediately became greatly exasperated and struck him savagely with a shovel twice, knocking him down, and inflicting a wound on the head from which the blood flowed copiously, as can be testified so by several eye-witnesses. At the same time he remarked angrily, "I'll kill you next time!"

Said Ramon Johnson had been at school but a short time, and was a well-behaved boy. We earnestly request that investigation be made in regard to this matter, which is a glaring outrage on humanity, as well as a conspicuous breach of discipline. Being moreover a menace to our personal safety, we ask that protective measures be taken in our behalf.

The tyrannical and overbearing conduct of said McCowan has caused great dissatisfaction and a general feeling of depression throughout the school, and consequently a source of much discouragement among the children, preventing them taking due interest in their studies and occupations.

This cruel and cowardly act has set before the school a melancholy example of injustice and oppression.

[To save space, a complaint about irregular payment of the children's wages has been deleted.]

Moreover the discipline has been greatly modified during the administration of Supt. McCowan, and exercises in military tactics are no longer given, as was the case under the former administration of Mr. Hall.

Neither have we any commanding officer to instruct us in same, since the removal of Capt. Wickham.

It is to be greatly regretted that these desirable and useful methods of instruction should be compelled to give way to others entirely outside the requirements for instruction prescribed by the Government, and which we regard as pernicious.

A dancing master and class is a recent innovation to which we strenuously object from conscientious and moral motives. Until recently it was customary to permit visitors to attend without special invitation, resulting in the introduction of a class of young men of doubtful morality, who came for the purpose of dancing immodestly with the Indian girls. it is believed that visitors are now mainly restricted to those receiving special invitations, but the dance is still detestable and unseemly to us. We regard it as immoral, and protest against the undue pressure brought to bear on the Indian children to participate, the girls being sometimes severely scolded if they refuse to do so, and as a consequence some of them are found weeping bitterly, at the conclusion of the dance at the outrage imposed on their maidenly modesty.

Being lovers of sociality we much regret the loss of the former pleasant evenings under the administration of the last Superintendent, spent in social intercourse, merriment, and address.

Recognizing the large expenditure of money in appropriations etc. which the magnanimity of the Government has conferred in our interests, we wish to show our appreciation of the same by loyalty and patriotism and by endeavoring to advance in the ways of civilization, to increase our knowledge, and learn the arts of industry and peace.

But need we protest that it is not possible to take the interest in these things which we should desire, when we feel our Superintendent has no sympathy for, and but little interest in us? If it is through his instrumentality that said appropriations have been made, we would give honor to whom honor is due, and were it possible would fain believe that he is actuated by motives of philanthropy and affection, for a hitherto oppressed and unfortunate people, rather than by those inspired by ambition, selfishness and pride.

And in view of the foregoing reasons, we earnestly pray for the re-instation of Mr. Howard Hall, our former Superintendent, a man of high principles, integrity, and honor, a man who favored religious instruction, sympathizing deeply with the Indians, and interesting himself magnanimously in their behalf, a man who was everywhere by the whites respected and esteemed, and by the Indians universally beloved.

We earnestly entreat your careful consideration of our petition, and have confidence to believe that by a Government based upon the principles of right and equity, in whom alone we have hope of redress, it will not be disregarded.

---

*Robert A. Trennert is professor of history at Arizona State University.*

# Saddle Strings in the Books

*Nellie E. Shaver

In a little valley in northern Arizona I attended my first school. Money had been raised by giving dances and the lumber had been hauled from the mill by a freighter who made no charge for the use of his team. The carpenter work was also given and a strong but rough little house had been put up. It was not lined or papered on the inside or painted anywhere; the rough frame served as shelves for a few books and the crayon for our blackboard which was made of two wide boards painted black.

The desks and benches were home made and had a strong inclination to tip over if we got up in a hurry when a class was called. There were from five to seven pupils, five being necessary to keep up the district. Our teachers usually came to us from California, ambitious girls from the state normal pushing out for the larger wages given in Arizona, or some man attracted by the still larger salaries paid to men.

Certainly the road to learning was not made easy or particularly pleasant; we had none of the tools of a modern school room but had the "Three R's" drilled into us in the most monotonous way. Arithmetic was always the important thing, especially if we had a man teacher, and I was taught no grammar at all till I entered the school at Prescott.

Most of the pupils rode to school on gentle old cow ponies and a good part of the noon hour was taken up in watering the horses and staking them in a new place on fresh grass. We also dug in the Indian graves which were all around the school house, or went up on a hill crowned with a small prehistoric ruin and hunted for arrowheads and bits of colored pottery. None of us knew anything about these things and our teachers could not tell us much for the ruins of the Southwest were then but little explored. One man teacher found us so uninteresting that on warm days he used to go to sleep between classes, having tacked up a large sheet of brown paper on the rough wall so he could lean back in his chair and doze without the splinters pulling his hair. The boys more often than not wore their chaps—the leather leggins of the cowboys—to school but took them off and hung them on the wall till time to go home.

When I came to go to school at Prescott there was no high school but in one room a high school course was given—the same room in which Jessie Benton Fremont used to come on Fridays to give talks on history and tell of her European travels, while Governor Fremont was governor of Arizona. In this room hung a large picture of Governor Safford who has well been called the "Father of the Arizona Public Schools."

At that time several of my fellow pupils were working, as I was, to pay for lodging and the chance to go to school. Students worked desperately hard for what education they got and many a text book was marked in the middle with saddle strings where it was tied to the saddle to be studied on herd behind the cattle or on the road going and coming to school.

---

**Taken from* The Arizona Journal of Education *October 1910, p. 46, and June 1911, pp. 76-77. It was credited to "Miss Shauer," a teacher in Phoenix's first school. Phoenix records show Nellie E. Shaver teaching in the Little Adobe School in 1873.*

# Glimpses: the 1800s

## THE TEACHER'S VIEW OF ARIZONA'S FIRST PUBLIC SCHOOL
### John A. Spring

I think this day was the second Monday in the month of March, 1871. On the first day, nearly 100 boys were enrolled, and on the closing of the lists on the third day the names enrolled numbered 138. Of all of these boys, of whom a few showed already a forthcoming beard, while others could barely manage to climb upon the benches, not one could express himself intelligently in the English language; about five or six understood sufficient English to know what to do when asked . . . . I therefore, explained everything in Spanish, the boys' mother tongue, so that every sentence that was translated or read or spoken in English was immediately conveyed to their intellect in a comprehensible manner. The school was taught from 8 a.m. to 12 and from 1 p.m. to 4 p.m . . . . Upon opening the school in the morning, one hour was devoted to penmanship . . . . Governor Safford had kindly presented to the school two dozen Ollendorff's grammars for the use of the boys who could read Spanish fluently and write without difficulty. To those boys whom I formed into a class I would, after they had written a page in their copy books, read and thoroughly explain a lesson in Ollendorff and show them how to translate the Spanish exercises properly into English which they immediately did in writing . . . . The Ollendorff class soon became very proficient and fairly doted on the little stories in the first and second readers . . . . The afternoon was generally devoted to figures, and twice a week I gave all the boys a drawing lesson which all of them considered a perfect treat.

*John A. Spring presented these memories before a Territorial Teachers Institute held on December 31, 1897. This quote was taken from* The Historical Role of Arizona's Superintendent of Public Instruction *by John C. Bury (Flagstaff: Northern Arizona University, 1974): Vol. l, pp. 74-75.*

## A SPIKY-TAILED INTERRUPTION

I furnished a good deal of amusement for my school today quite unexpectedly. I was hearing a geography lesson when I felt something tugging at my dress and felt a weight which I shook off. Presently feeling it again, I looked down and there lying on my dress skirt in a ray of sunlight was a hideous big reptile, black and yellow like a lizard, with a "spiky" tail and a head like a snake and over a foot long. I gathered up my dress and with a yell that could have been heard a mile, I jumped upon the stool I had been sitting on. Ida and Laura looked at the thing and promptly followed my example; the littlest children cried with fright at our strange antics, but when the boys saw the creature they laughed and said, "Why teacher, that's nothing but a Gila Monster."

I jumped off the stool on the side away from the monster and gave a sudden recess while I asked for information. The children said some folks thought the Gila Monster was poison and that he could "blow himself up with wind and puff it in your face and make you awful sick." In the meantime, our Gila Monster had walked to a hole near my desk and gone down it to his own quarters, and we took up our work again as quietly as possible.

*This excerpt was published under the heading "Some Early Arizona Schools" in* The Arizona Journal of Education *June, 1911, pp. 77-78. The writer was identified only as an early teacher in one of the remote mountain districts of Arizona.*

## OF TALCUM POWDER AND INDIAN DRILLS

In 1881, Clara Stillman came from Bridgeport to become Bisbee's first school teacher. An old miner's shack with no doors, windows, or even a floor served as the schoolhouse. The teacher's desk was a flour barrel turned upside down. The students' desks were made from boards resting on packing boxes; seats were planks nailed on kegs.

The desks were so rough that pen and ink could hardly be used and so most of the writing was done on slates that sold for about 75 cents. Pencils cost 25 cents. The blackboards were made of smooth boards nailed together and painted black. Since there was seldom any chalk, talcum powder was used.

During these school days, instead of holding fire drills, the town held Indian drills. When the whistle at the hoisting works was blown four times—two short, one long, and one short—women and children were to dash to shelter in the mine tunnel.

*Adapted from* Arizona, a Short History *by Obie B. Faulk, University of Oklahoma Press, 1970.*

## THE DROPPING IN OF THE SCHOOL SUPERINTENDENT

County school superintendents were famous for dropping in for unexpected visits to local schools, but according to a diary left by a teacher near Prescott, the "dropping in" almost became literal.

"We discovered," she wrote, "that our little log school house was infested with a large gray woodtick, so we moved our school out under some scrub oak bushes, but as the windy season came on we had to find better quarters. There was in the school yard a large hole where someone had started to dig a well. It was fifteen feet deep and had so caved in that it was about the same width. One of the boys dug some rude steps, and in this impromptu school house we were finishing the term. The county superintendent, coming to visit our school, heard voices but saw no one, and as he was about to fall in on our school, I bade him come down. After holding a little examination, he christened this the banner school of the county."

*As quoted by Jennie Ellingson in "The Growth of the Arizona Public School System up to the Year 1876,"* The Arizona Journal of Education, *October, 1919.*

## THE OLD TUBAC SCHOOL
### Elizabeth R. Brownell

On December 1, 1876, twelve petitioners filed for the establishment of Tubac School District No. 4 with boundaries "as follows, to wit: the valley of the Santa Cruz river lying south of Tubac." The school undoubtedly grew slowly. As late as 1884, the teacher, Sarah M. Black and her students could fit into one end of T. Little Mercer's store. In 1885, Mr. Mercer built the Old Tubac School, which was in use until 1965 and is now part of the Tubac Presidio State Historic Park. The original schoolroom with its slate blackboards and desk chairs is on exhibit.

By the 1890s, school records show between 117 to 140 pupils with usually three teachers and an appropriation from the state of $1,500. Few teachers were named in the district records, although in 1898 Carmen Garcia was identified as being paid $3.00 per month for janitor services, Samuel Kaphan received $5.00 and $6.00 for delivering wood to the school, and supply warrants for $25.00 and $5.25 were sent to W. B. Pierce and a Mrs. Mansfeld.

In the summer of 1899, the new Board of Examiners recommended that the license of the current teacher be revoked after he failed to appear before them to defend himself on charges of "immoral and unprofessional conduct" and that "he was much addicted to the use of intoxicating liquors." Old timers recall that even in his previous job as Justice of the Peace the man had been known for his drinking.

The teacher hired to replace him was Della Johnson. In 1960, she wrote a letter to Frank Griffin in which she stated:

> I am Della Johnson who taught school in Tubac at the turn of the century and I remember very well the people and the buildings. The old Fort was standing then. We had a one-room schoolhouse and a church. The Burruel family was the most important and influential family . . . . I knew Anna A. Pugh [the teacher who succeeded Della Johnson in 1902-03]. I also remember the ranchers in the area including Mr. George Atkinson, Morgan and Joe Wise. There was no railroad through Tubac and I rode in and out on a stagecoach . . . . I have lived in Indiana 58 years, but I never lost my feelings for Arizona . . . . I look at Westerns on television just to see the desert and cactus.

Della Johnson left after her marriage to a Mr. Welcher who was employed by the George B. Marsh Hardware Company in Nogales. The Anna Pugh, whom she mentions as her successor, did not stay and was replaced by James Cowan who taught until 1905 when he combined being teacher with being postmaster. Luisa Yoas of Tubac remembers Mr. Cowan as having only one arm. He spoke and wrote good Spanish, she says, and was often called upon to translate. In view of the fact that nearly all the students were Mexican, it would seem to have been helpful to have a bilingual teacher, but this qualification was rarely considered necessary.

*Elizabeth R. Brownell has compiled a history of Tubac 1853-1980 which is to be published by Westernlore Press in Tucson. The above material was adapted from her manuscript.*

## FROM A BARRICADE TO A FLOWER GARDEN
### Irene A. Kennedy

In 1873, my father was thirteen-years-old when his family came west from Ohio on the Union Pacific. He told me that he had finished *McGuffey's Fifth Reader*

Creighton School in Phoenix, 1891. *Arizona Historical Foundation photo.*

which is the way children were graded then. This was considered adequate schooling, and when the family went to Santa Barbara he got a job setting type for the local newspaper. He loved to read and became a self-educated man. In 1880, he came to Arizona and lived in the San Simon Valley and the Chiricahua Mountains of southeastern Arizona.

My mother's father had a ranch three miles from Fort Grant. This was in the 1880s and there were no schools. A man in poor health came to the home of my grandfather, Miles L. Wood. Grandfather told this man he could stay and teach his three little girls. My mother was the oldest.

By the time the man left, Mother was in the third grade. Then her father had the three girls ride to Fort Grant to go to school with the officers' children. Two girls rode a horse and the other one a mule. Then my grandfather built an adobe room on his land for a school house for the children of the little town of Bonita. The teacher usually boarded at Grandfather's home. His house was a large eleven-room building shaped around a square courtyard. It was shaped this way so the horses could be put inside and the entrance blocked to keep people from stealing the horses. At one time, two families were barricaded in the house. Mother remembered hearing shots from Indians and soldiers who were fighting. Later this courtyard became grandmother's flower garden.

*Irene A. Kennedy graduated from Tempe Normal School in 1920 with a life-time teaching certificate.*

## ELOCUTION VS. MATHEMATICS
### Margaret Hurley

I went to school at the convent, located on Monroe a block west of St. Mary's, until I finished the fourth grade. The first day in school [1895], I was punished for talking—I didn't know that I was supposed to stop talking when school began. When I didn't stop, the sister came and slapped my hand with the belt of her robe. She also told me to go and stand in the corner. I was very much ashamed, especially when one of the big boys made fun of me.

I didn't get a firm grounding in arithmetic because I was good in elocution and had to practice my recitations when the elocution teacher came during arithmetic periods. Our school had a "concert" every spring and everyone practiced very hard. I recited selections like "The Eagle's Nest" and "Curfew Shall Not Ring

Tonight." About a week before the concert, the sisters would line us up, two by two, and we would march from school to Patton's Opera House that stood on the corner of Central and Jefferson, across from the present Luhrs Hotel. We had our "dress rehearsals" on the Opera House stage.

The summer after I finished fourth grade, a woman from back east (she was a school teacher) boarded at the ranch and tutored us children. She discovered how poorly prepared I was in arithmetic, and after that mother decided no more elocution. In the fall I went to public school— the East End Elementary School.

Washington Street was not paved when I was a child. When it rained, it was a sea of mud. We did not go to the grocery store in those days; instead, the groceryman rode his bicycle out to our ranch once a week to get mother's order. We bought our vegetables from a Chinese man who drove around in a covered wagon. I liked to climb up under the canvas to see what he had for sale. It was always a happy day when he had hubbard squash—mother liked to cook it for us.

I remember the delicious apples and peaches that were grown in Oak Creek. I don't remember that we had ice to begin with, but later I can remember driving in the surrey to the ice factory on East Washington and bringing home a block of ice for the refrigerator.

*Margaret Hurley wrote this memory for the Pioneer Biography Project of the Arizona Historical Foundation.*

## SHARLOT HALL'S "LOTS OF WORK AND LITTLE SCHOOLING"

In February of 1882, Sharlot Hall, who was to grow up to become one of Arizona's best known writers and historians, arrived with her parents in the Agua Fria Valley near Prescott. She was eleven years old and later said about the period, "Our lives were like those of all families on the small ranches—lots of work and little schooling or other opportunities . . . . I studied mostly at home, between whiles of watering or herding the cattle."

In a 1911 interview with the *Arizona Republican*, Sharlot said that in this "little log and slab and stone and adobe schoolhouse" she and her brother "sat on wooden benches, without desks enough to go around, and wrote lessons on the red felt edged slates that were counted a riotous luxury—for plain wooden framed slates were the usual thing."

In a later interview published in the October 1924 *Yavapai Magazine*, Sharlot stated:

> I wrote my first book of verse in one of the little yellow paper backed-notebooks, called "The Farmer's and Mechanic's Note Book" and sent out yearly by some patent medicine company . . . .
>
> This "first edition" showed my early historical bent for it contained verses about the discovery of Florida, about Columbus, and all sorts of ballads about Indian fights and frontier life. It was largely written when I was supposed to be laboring with my geography lesson—but that study was such fun for me that one reading "got" a lesson and I generally could reel off all the reading matter in the book "by heart."

Teachers seldom stayed at these little country schools more than a year or two. The only one of Sharlot's teachers identified by name was Miss Neenah Johnson, who taught the 1885-86 term. During this year, Sharlot's father was a school trustee, and at the end of the year was thanked for loaning his military uniform and gun for a school skit.

In her later life, Sharlot characterized her father as anti-intellectual and hostile toward "book learning." But apparently Miss Johnson was successful in convincing Jim Hall that Sharlot should have further education. In October of 1866, Sharlot enrolled for her final year of schooling in Prescott. She lived with a family and worked for her board and room. Her father worried that she would "git high toned and think she's above us."

Sharlot made friends with Ida Williams, who many years later said she would never forget the fiery poetry recitations that Sharlot practiced for elocution. "The old pieces in Appleton's Fifth Reader were certainly made to yield every shade of meaning."

Another friend that Sharlot made that year was the elderly Henry W. Fleury, who had come to Prescott in 1864 as private secretary to Arizona's first territorial governor, John N. Goodwin. Fleury lived in the old Governor's Mansion and entertained Sharlot with stories of his own pioneer days, which probably added to Sharlot's interest in history.

*Adapted from* A Passion for Freedom: The Life of Sharlot Hall *by Margaret Maxwell (University of Arizona Press, 1982).*

## CAMPING OUT FOR SCHOOL

Jane Fourr was one of the many Arizona pioneer women who, although they lived on isolated cattle ranches, wanted their children to go to school. In a biography written by Mary R. Coolidge, Fourr's neighbors describe her as a submissive woman who devotedly catered to her husband's needs. Nevertheless, in spite of his opposition to their children attending school, Jane Fourr took this one decision to be hers.

Every summer she and the older children worked hard on the ranch. In the fall—no matter what "Mister Fourr" said—they loaded a few necessities into wagons and drove to Tombstone, where Jane rented some empty house in which they half-lived, half-camped during the school year. Old timers in Tombstone said that the Fourr children and their mother came to town in this fashion for fifteen years. [*Arizona Quarterly* 1:3 (1945) p. 32.]

*Told by Christiane Fischer in "A Profile of Women in Arizona in Frontier Days,"* JOURNAL OF THE WEST *July, 1977, p. 45.*

## LEARNING ON THE LITTLE COLORADO
### Blonda Bushman Yount

Very early in 1876, the Church of Jesus Christ of Latter Day Saints headquartered in Salt Lake City, Utah called about two hundred of its members to go to the Little Colorado Valley for the purpose of colonization. Here between the Painted Desert and the mountain tops has been enacted a chapter in western history. To protect themselves from Indians, the pioneers built a rock fort in which to live. The land was parched and dry and no crops could be raised without irrigation water. The men built a diversion dam across the Little Colorado River, but by July summer floods washed the dam away. Fifteen times these industrious people built dams, and fifteen times they were washed away before they finally had one that would hold.

My grandfather, John Bushman, was one of these pioneers and served as community leader and Bishop of the church from 1887 to 1916. The first year there were only two or three children in the fort so no school was held. But the second year they started a "day school." My grandfather served on the Board of Education for the Little Colorado area and with others started the Snowflake Academy with forty-four students. Each ward (town) donated $1,000 to the building of the Academy, which was founded in 1891. This was like a high school, and students would go to Snowflake and board with families so they could get an education beyond that offered in elementary schools throughout Navajo County.

Snowflake Academy. *Arizona Historical Foundation photo.*

Joseph City was originally named St. Joseph to honor Joseph Smith, the founder of the Mormon Church. Included in the original families whose names are still common in the area were Richards, Porter, Tanner, Allen, Randall, Westover, Smith, and Turley. St. Joseph was the first permanent settlement in the Little Colorado Valley and is now a thriving community with a full elementary and high school.

When I attended school there in the 1920s, many community events were held at the school including the regular Saturday night dance. We still had no high school, and students were transported to Holbrook in a specially constructed panel truck. Here I was introduced to working in a chemistry lab, typing and editing a school newspaper, playing a violin in the school orchestra, being a member of a debating team, and participating in voice competitions and operettas. Looking back, it now seems insignificant, but in 1929 it was very important to me to be chosen valedictorian of the Holbrook High School graduating class which consisted of twelve students.

*Blonda Bushman Yount went on to graduate from Arizona State Teachers' College in 1934 and to teach in Eloy and Glendale. She now lives in Laguna Niguel, California and is a well known artist.*

## 88 YEARS IN THE SAME SCHOOL
### Rose Faras

In 1893, my parents moved from Phoenix to Tempe where my father was janitor for a brief period in Tempe Normal School. We returned to Phoenix in 1896. My sister, Concepcion (Connie), my two brothers, and I attended the West End School in Phoenix. There were only three schools in the city: the West End School, the East End School, and the Central School.

I have a picture of my second-grade class with thirty-three students. One of the students I recognize is Kathryn Osborn, sister of former Governor Sidney Osborn. Miss Mills was the teacher. She was a wonderful teacher loved by all her students.

In those days, students received monthly report cards to be signed by parents and returned to the teacher. Grades were listed in all subjects taught, number of days attended during the month, days absent, number of times the student was late to school, and even a grade in deportment.

Our next move was to Douglas, a new smelter town on the Mexican border in the southeast corner of the state. A new school was just being built for grades five through high school.

*Both sisters graduated from Douglas High School, attended Tempe Normal, and returned to Douglas where Connie began teaching in the Pirtleville School in 1913 and Rose in 1917. They both served as principal with Connie retiring in 1957 and Rose in 1961. On July 1, 1980, the name of the school was changed from Pirtleville to Faras in honor of the 88 years of teaching that the two sisters did in the same school. As Rose Faras said when she wrote the above statement on June 28, 1984, "The greatest reward for a teacher is the success of her pupils. Many of our students continued their education. Among them are teachers, principals, dentists, engineers, lawyers, court interpreters, and one former governor, Raul Castro."*

Wickenburg's one-room schoolhouse was brought from the Vulture Mine in 1895. Ann Purdy, owner of this photo taken in 1903, remembers posing in front of the only unbroken window. Related story on pages 133-34.

# 1900-1919: Statehood Days

Between 1900 and 1919, both the Mexican and Russian Revolutions occurred and so did World War I—the war to end all wars. The first radio programs were broadcast, the Panama Canal was built, and 500,000 Americans died in the great flu epidemic. The Carnegie Foundation set aside 125 million dollars for education, and Congress passed the Eighteenth Amendment ushering in a decade of prohibition.

Visitors as well as settlers streamed into Arizona on the newly built railroads. When the first major dam of the Salt River Project was completed, Theodore Roosevelt came to speak at its dedication. The completion of the dam and its storage reservoir meant that the necessary water could be provided for agriculture and mining, and Arizona's population could grow accordingly. The celebration was a forerunner to Statehood Day, celebrated less than a year later on February 14, 1912.

Between 1900 and 1912, the school age population increased from 17,716 to 42,318. Average daily attendance was only slightly over half these figures. In 1900, the average length of the school year was approximately six months for which male teachers were paid $81.00 a month, with female teachers receiving $65.00. Teachers' pay climbed steadily until in 1911-1912 men were getting $118.00 per month and women $82.00. The next year, pay for men took a ten-dollar drop, perhaps in response to women's requests for equal pay. Instead of raising the women's pay, however, most school boards lowered the men's pay. There were 120 male teachers compared to 757 female teachers. Reforms toward equal pay turned out to be short-lived. By the end of this period, the 1919-20 school year, men were earning $165.00 per month while women were earning $119.00.

Other money-related issues of the early 1900s included a dispute in northern Arizona with the Santa Fe Pacific Railroad which refused to pay school taxes. In areas of wide open spaces, it was often the railroads or the mines that provided nearly the total school budget. In 1900 the Northern Arizona County Supervisors, instead of taking the railroad to court, arranged a compromise allowing the company to pay only a percentage of its taxes. The following year schools in these counties had money to operate for only three months.

Especially prior to statehood, school financing was a major problem. In his annual report for 1900, the superintendent of Navajo County recommended that temporary certificates no longer be issued because district trustees waited until the last possible moment and then hired unqualified, and therefore cheaper teachers for whom they could get temporary certificates. In Cochise County, the mines hired children who should still be in school, prompting the Territorial Legislature of 1907 to pass a child labor law. That year 5,166 school age children had not attended any school. The mines also hired away the teachers giving them better salaries and even better working conditions.

In 1908, Territory Superintendent Robert Lindley Long made a plea for increasing the salaries of teachers in order to get well trained professionals who would stay in their jobs. The turn-over rate for Arizona teachers was extremely high because teachers were constantly jockeying for better paying jobs. Many came west for an adventure or vacation while others came in hopes that the climate would improve their poor health.

Eighth grade graduation in St. Johns, 1915.

Tempe Union High School girls' basketball team, 1911. *Tempe Historical Museum photo.*

Ida Slade Burgess at Northern Arizona Normal School, 1918.

Dos Cabezas at the turn of the century. *Arizona Historical Foundation photo.*

Tempe Public School Baseball Team, 1917. *Tempe Historical Museum photo.*

Superintendent Long recommended that districts try to hire graduates of Arizona schools.

Long's report of 1906 showed that 50% of the school age children in the territory spoke Spanish. All reports of the period showed a lower level of achievement for Spanish speaking children; several mentioned the desirability of hiring bilingual teachers. Alfred Ruiz, Apache County Superintendent, expressed the opinion that the normal schools had a responsibility to prepare bilingual teachers. Robert C. Smith of Navajo County recommended that Mexican children be separated from "white" children. He added that he had already taken steps to do this in Winslow and Silver Creek.

During this same time period, the Douglas and Phoenix school districts took it upon themselves to segregate black students, and the Territorial legislature subsequently passed a law saying that when the number of black students exceeded eight in a school district they were to be segregated and provided with an equal education. A case was brought before the State Supreme Court in July of 1912. The law was upheld, but the particular children involved were allowed to attend the white school nearer their home. The judge ruled they were not being given equality when they had to cross two railroad tracks and travel further than the "children of said district of the same grade who were not of the African race." Four decades later, the state law was changed.

A more positive development of the pre-statehood era was the establishment of high schools. As early as 1881 a report of the United States Commissioner of Education mentioned high school work in Tucson, Prescott, and Phoenix. Tombstone was also known to have high school work in the early 1880s. However it wasn't until N. J. Netherton, Territorial Superintendent of Public Instruction made his report for 1893-94, that the creation of high schools was formally proposed. The 1895 Territorial Assembly passed a law stating that high schools could be formed by districts with a minimum of 2,000 residents. Phoenix was the first to take advantage of the new legislation, opening a high school in 1895, followed by Mesa in 1901, Prescott in 1903, and Morenci and Clifton in 1904. Tucson did not begin a high school until 1906 because for fifteen years its young people had been enrolled in the University's preparatory department. By 1911, high schools had also been established in Tempe, Bisbee, Douglas, Tombstone, and Globe. In 1912 the law was liberalized so that smaller communities, if they had adequate funding, could also open high schools. By 1918, Arizona had over thirty high schools, eight accredited by the North Central Association: Bisbee, Globe, Mesa, Phoenix, Prescott, Thatcher (The Gila Academy), Tucson, and Winslow.

The Arizona constitution gave the legislature power to establish a uniform school system beginning with kindergarten. Special categories included normal schools, universities, industrial schools, and schools for the deaf, dumb, and blind. Of great importance to the new state was the granting by the federal government of ten million acres of land for the support of schools.

Under the new constitution, Charles O. Case was the first elected Superintendent of Public Instruction. Between 1912 and 1921, he championed the cause of the classroom teacher, worked for better physical conditions for children especially in the rural schools, encouraged standardization and improvement of teacher certification requirements, and supported efforts to make schools serve practical, everyday needs by providing communities with libraries and industrial education programs. He helped to get the 1918 Legislature to pass a bill providing night schools to teach English to non-native speakers. He also helped pass a bill allowing districts to hold part-time schools for working children between the ages of fourteen and sixteen. The law required employers to give children time off to attend such schools.

These twenty years were a time of steady growth for Arizona schools. The lack of money was somewhat eased by the growth in population and by the ruling that federal lands could be leased for the support of schools. Major accomplishments included the establishment of high schools and the general acceptance of the necessity to support education beyond the typical elementary and high schools. Issues still unresolved from this period include questions related to segregation; bilingual education; equality of employment opportunities for females, and local control vs. state control.

# From a Noisy Fire Wagon to a Silent Armistice

Dorothy Robinson

*Arizona Historical Foundation photo.*

I was born in Phoenix on East Adams Street in 1898. I think one of my earliest memories is when I retreated to safety behind the screen door to watch a three-horse team come dashing up the street, pulling a smoke-belching fire engine—the good old fashioned kind. The sight was terrifying in a delicious way.

I attended the first and second grades at the old Central School in Phoenix, which used to be near Van Buren and First Streets. I have a mental picture of myself standing with other first graders waiting for a President of the Unites States to pass. I was not so much concerned with seeing the great man as with waving my little flag properly. If I used a circular motion it wrapped around the stick, but if I jerked it back and forth, the stars and stripes did not show.

Phoenix was a small town where horse-drawn sprinklers tried to keep down the dust most of the year. We children loved to let water from the wagons splash on our legs. Nothing much could be done about the deep mud that followed rains.

One time the trustees of the school paid their annual visit to the grades. My father was one of them, so I cheerfully said "Hello, Papa," and was reprimanded when I reached home that evening. That was not the thing to do.

About this time I learned to ride a bicycle. Everybody did. I got on safely and could ride, but didn't know how to get off, so I rode and rode and rode around and around the block until I was exhausted and fell off. So I learned how.

I didn't have much trouble learning to read. One day we were told to study a certain page. I can still see it. There was a picture—black and white of course—of a tree on the upper half and below that ten or twelve lines of print. After a little while I raised my hand to announce that I could read it. The teacher said, "Good, now let's see if you can read it backward." In my memory I can see my finger conscientiously pointing to each word in reverse order. I was quite pleased when I knew each one.

My parents had advanced ideas about education and began my piano lessons when I was about seven. There was also an opportunity for me to take French. I can remember sitting in front of a bright Navajo rug and naming the colors and also talking about the "pen of my aunt." That all stopped when we moved out to my uncle's ranch when I was nine. There was no school near enough for small children to attend. Mother had been a teacher and father was interested in education so for a while we were taught at home. Mother usually read aloud in the evenings, and as there were few other diversions we children read any and every thing we could.

By the time I was in the fifth grade, my parents thought I was old enough to ride with my little brother the four or five miles to Creighton School. We had a safe old horse that never ran away except when a motorcycle came by. But that spurt of energy didn't last long. For family transportation we had a buggy pulled by Elizabeth, a rather homely old mare, white with plenty of speckles. When excited she would just go to pieces and sit down. When that happened, the harness had to be freed from the vehicle, which was pushed back. Then Elizabeth was calmed, helped to her feet, and reharnessed.

It was inconvenient and at times exciting to have this happen. Once on the desert when she saw a rattlesnake she sat down. Another time in Phoenix she was on the streetcar track, and the motorman clanged the bell at her. Again her hind legs gave way and down she went. Mother came home full of remarks about being put in such an embarrassing position.

Otherwise Elizabeth was most reliable. When the ranch cook quit, he drove her in to Phoenix. Then he found someone to take his place, put the new cook in the buggy, headed Elizabeth east on McDowell Road and told the new cook not to get out until the horse stopped in a barnyard. That would be where he was going to work.

When I was in eighth grade my brother and I attended a school just two miles west of our home. It had one room and was run by the Seventh Day Adventists. The classes started with Bible reading, mostly their interpretation of the Book of Revelations. Each evening the family carefully relieved our minds of the fears engendered by the morning lesson.

It was here that I had my first and only fight in school. A big boy picked on my little brother. I rushed in and hit and punched vigorously. I have a feeling that the fight was short and that I won because of his surprise and my fury. I don't remember whether the affair was discussed at home.

My first year at the Normal School I lived in East Hall. Room and board cost $26.00 per month. I loved dormitory life, but it was nice to go home every third week. Of course I came in a horse and buggy. Mother usually drove me over. We forded the river most of the time. Once the water was so high I had to take my suitcase and walk across on the railroad bridge. When I heard a train coming I stepped off on one of the big supporting pillars as it went by. I wish I could dramatize incidents and make them exciting, but they usually seem matter of fact to me.

I was not particularly brilliant in school. I liked to write even then and was a minor reporter on the paper and did work on the annual. I was rereading it the other day and noticed that my favorite recreation was supposed to be working arithmetic, which brought to mind that as a student teacher I taught eighth grade arithmetic for Mr. Payne and had to work the problems first and get the correct answers. It took me hours and hours.

In those days we student taught for an hour a day for four quarters. In that way we had experiences in four different areas. Mine were in eighth grade arithmetic, seventh grade geography, second grade arithmetic, and another quarter in the primary department.

With only an hour a day it was very difficult to get a feeling of rapport with the class and establish any discipline. Two things I remember from teaching for Mr. Payne: In disciplinary matters the individual offender is the one who should be punished, and bits of paper on the floor make an unattractive schoolroom. I followed those two suggestions all the years I taught.

In 1916 we were graduated. I remember I was exhausted from all the festivities. Mother and I went up to our cabin on the western edge of Prescott in a little development named Pine Crest. There we just ate and slept for a week.

My first teaching position was in Chandler in an intermediate grade. I had a terrible time with discipline. Merton Rice, my first principal, was very nice and helped me out time after time. I dreamed of teaching all night and would awaken and get up to do various tasks I would think of. Eventually I got to have pretty good order.

I taught in Chandler all during World War I. I headed the local Junior Red Cross and we knit sweaters like mad. My mother was manager at the San Marcos. It was a winter resort hotel where people came and settled down for weeks. Everyone was knitting, so we worked out a plan where I cut heavy wire into knitting-needle lengths and sharpened a point on one end. Then the ladies at the hotel set up sleeveless sweaters on pairs of needles and the children in my class finished them. It seems to me that we produced 100 sweaters that winter.

A big wooden box was delivered to my room for the sweaters to be packed in. It was as big as my desk and had a heavy wooden cover resting on top. One day we came in from the playground. I started the class on some written work, and then because I had had a vigorous workout I leaned against the box and then hopped up a little to sit on the lid, which was not fastened securely. My feet were off the floor so when the cover tipped down I went with it until only my feet showed. There was a deathly silence for a minute, then the class shouted and yelled with laughter as I slowly pulled myself out.

Those five-and-a-half-years teaching in Chandler were very good. I loved horseback riding. And there were picnics and dances. Some dances were held in the ballroom of the San Marcos, others in less pretentious structures in the surrounding towns. All were fun.

There were picture shows too. One picture was scheduled that I wanted to see, but I had to finish a sweater, so I took it and tried to knit by feel in the dark theater. By the end of the show I could knit without looking, but you should have seen the sweater. It had to be redone.

The schools were closed during the flu epidemic in 1918. I worked in the garden at San Marcos, digging out weeds mostly, at 25 cents an hour and earned about $25.00.

In Chandler the way to notify people of newsworthy events was to ring the school bell. But in November 1918 the school house was being used as a hospital and was filled with flu patients. The doctors wouldn't let anyone ring the bell. Therefore we in town did not know when the Armistice had been signed. We never did get to have a noisy celebration.

---

*Dorothy Robinson wrote these memories in 1969 when items were being gathered for placement in an ASU College of Education time capsule.*

---

## A PLAYGROUND ON THE ROOF

Roberta Watt Troxell

School in Morenci was in session as early as 1890. Carrie N. Hunt taught that year in a one-room school provided by the Detroit Company. During the 1890s, school was conducted in various places including a lodging house. In 1902 the Detroit Company and the Arizona Copper Company constructed a one-story school. Later a second story was added to the building known as the Longfellow School. Dr. James Douglas provided books for a school library.

The first high school enrolled one pupil in 1902. She was Mirna Robison, who graduated in 1906 and came back to Morenci to teach until her retirement. The concept of bilingual education is not as new as people may think. In 1906-07 an evening school provided classes for Spanish speakers who wanted to learn English as well as for English speakers who wanted to learn Spanish.

Flat, open spaces have always been hard to find in Morenci, and one of the early elementary schools was built with a children's playground on the roof. That school, along with the rest of Old Morenci, is no more, having been taken over by the open pit mine.

*Roberta Watt Troxell, who lives in the "new" Morenci, wrote a master's thesis on the history of Morenci in 1956.*

---

# Little Country Kids

Chrystle Willis Ross

I was born Chrystle Marietta Willis in Granite Dells in the year 1894. I wasn't quite six years old when we moved to Phoenix and I started school.

We were all little country kids and we looked alike. Our mothers sewed our clothes, and there weren't many different patterns. Even the material was the same. A few town kids had better looking clothes. Girls wore pantywaists with garters to hold up their black hose, and black bloomers to cover the garters. Some of the kids had bloomers made out of flour sacks. We all wore black lace-up shoes.

The first school I attended was out in the country in the Cartwright District, northwest of Phoenix. It was all ranch area and we walked to school. Mothers and fathers didn't take time off from their chores to take us—we all had to walk. We had a big old school building, and all the grades were separated, each in a different room. The underside of the school was open, and during recess we played hide-and-go-seek among the foundation posts. The schoolyard was just bare dirt—no trees or anything.

The class was called the Chart Class, and there you learned the A,B,C's. I don't remember the teachers' names except Miss Lossing, the music teacher who would take me home every once in a while and give me a piece of cake or something.

Boys and girls all played together. I remember when I was in the Chart class, the big boys had killed a bullsnake in the yard, and they dared me to put it around my neck, which I did. It wasn't dead, and it wiggled off. I can still feel that thing slithering off my neck. I was sick for a week everytime I would think about it, but I showed those boys.

In the second grade I changed schools and went to one over on Grand Avenue. It was way out, almost out of the city limits. We lived on a homestead not too far from Grand Avenue, and our cousins lived on the next section. We had bikes and all rode to school together.

We all took our lunches. I can remember bread sandwiches with tomato preserves on them. I could hardly stand them, but I guess that was all Mama had to fix for us.

The railroad track went by that school, and sometimes the teacher would take us out to wave at the trains. One time she brought a box of pins and we each got to lay some on the track, crossed. After the train went over them, they were welded together and looked like scissors.

Then a school was built in the six-points area, about three miles from home. I would ride Old Ben. Dad would put the saddle on him because I was too small to do it for myself. Then off I'd go with Old Ben plodding right along. They had a place just out of the schoolyard to leave the horses tied up. Nobody ever bothered them. At lunch we would put a nosebag on them, and then give them water. One day as I was returning from school, I was reading and just letting Old Ben pick his own way home. He got too close to a telephone pole, and I ended up with a dislocated kneecap.

In the fourth grade I went to Central School. It was a big school located about where the broadcasting station is now in downtown Phoenix. We drove a buggy. Dad would hitch up the horse in the morning and we would drive to the livery stable where they cared for our animal until we returned from school. Just before school started, we all lined up — girls in one line and boys in another. The principal would play the Double Eagle by John Phillip Sousa on the gramophone, and we would march smartly into our classrooms.

Our school started at 8:00 a.m., but remember that

we were farm kids. If you were big enough to go to school, you were big enough to work. When I was seven, it was my job to get up first, start the fire in the cookstove, and do my share of the chores. By the time I was in the fourth grade, I was not only doing that, but feeding the animals, and milking my allowance of the dairy cows before I could leave for school. So I was always late.

The teacher thought that she could teach me to be on time by putting me in the cloakroom. Since I was late a lot, I spent many days in there. One morning I just marched out and went and got the buggy and drove home. When Mama saw me she said, "What are you doing home?" "Well," I said, "I didn't figure I was doing any good going to school and sitting in the cloakroom every day, so I just came home." She turned the buggy around and took me right back to school. She marched into the principal's office and told him what for. I never had to sit in the cloakroom again.

We didn't have much homework because as I said we all had farmwork to do. In school, we wrote on slates. The slates and the blackboard were used for all our figuring and practicing. Once in a while we got to use ink and paper. We each had an inkwell in our desk, and of course the boys put ink on the girls every chance they got. The lights at the schools were big oil lanterns that hung down. There was no running water. They drew the water out of the well in a bucket, and we had a community dipper.

We had spelling bees all the time. I remember that I got spelled down on *business*. I never forgot how to spell it after that. At recitation time, we had to read aloud for the teachers.

Every Friday was entertainment day. We had plays and general programs, and some of the kids sang or recited poems.

The boys and girls were separated on the playground at recess time. The boys played baseball, but we girls mostly played jacks and jumped rope. I could beat the boys playing marbles, so I often ended up on the boys' side, where I didn't belong. They really hated me for beating them. I had to give the marbles back, but I really had them worried.

We started school in September and got out the 29th of May. We had Christmas holiday. We had Valentine Parties and Easter celebrations, and a big Christmas party, and of course Halloween. I didn't get to participate in any of the things that were held after school. My folks sent us to learn, not to play. They felt the sports and clubs were a waste of time.

We studied the same things the kids do now—math,

First brick Cartwright School built in 1894 at 59th Avenue and Thomas Road. *Courtesy Cartwright District #83.*

history, geography and English. We didn't have an opportunity to study a foreign language in the first eight grades. We all spoke Mexican with the other kids from that segment of the community, so we didn't think there was any need to study another language in school.

The biggest difference in the schools then and now is that the teacher was the boss. She was in charge, and everyone obeyed her. She had the right to chastise and correct, and we knew it.

Most of my teachers were young, single women, but in the sixth and seventh grades I had a man teacher, Mr. Falcon. We moved to Buckeye, where Miss Lovejoy was in charge of teaching the little kids and he was in charge of teaching the older kids. It was a one-room school. They would take different groups of us different times of the day. When they were not working with us, we would just study. At the end of the week we would have a written examination. We could listen to the other grades, so when Mr. Falcon gave the tests, I would take both the sixth and seventh grade tests, thereby completing two grades in the same year. And by now I was old enough to drive the buggy to special things at the school, so I got to participate more. We next moved to Flagstaff where I attended the eighth grade. My favorite teacher there was Mr. Anderson. He was the principal, and taught some of the classes, and was very kind to all of us. In addition to the regular lessons, we had composition and music and home economics. We planned, cooked, and served a formal dinner for the school board. We set the table with linen and china. I had never done anything that fancy before.

In Flagstaff, it was about a mile to school from our house. The walks were made out of boards. We didn't wear slacks, and where the snow had not been cleared it would be above our knees. When we got to school our hose would be saturated — and our underclothes too, because we all wore long underclothes. When we would get to school, we would take off our hose and lay them on the radiator to dry. But our shoes were wet, and we just had to put them back on. When school was over we had to go through it all over again, yet we hardly ever had colds. The Gregg kids had to come into town from their ranch. They had a sled and a horse that brought them in, but in the fall and spring they could just walk.

I graduated from the eighth grade, but did not get to graduate with my class because I had diptheria and was out for quite a time. Graduation from eighth grade marked the end of regular education. Then you could go on to the college which was called Normal School. If you went for four years and did well, you could be a teacher. In the first eight grades, the district bought the school books and the students just borrowed them. But when you entered Normal School, you paid tuition and bought your own books. It was hard for my folks to come up with the money. And since I did not want to be a teacher anyway, I only went two years there.

All eight of the children in my parent's family went to Arizona schools and so did my three daughters. We all received good educations.

---

*Chrystle Willis Ross now lives in Covina, California with her daughter, Claudia Ross, who tells her own story in the 1940s chapter.*

---

## ADMISSION DAY IN JEROME

Francis R. Vihel

I was born in Jerome, Arizona Territory in 1905. That means I was almost seven years old when I participated in admission day exercises to celebrate the entrance of Arizona Territory into Statehood. It was Wednesday, February 14, 1912 when elementary school pupils of Jerome School District #9 assembled to commemorate Arizona becoming the forty-eighth State of the Union.

There was a patriotic speech delivered by the Honorable George W. Hull, the former Mayor, who was often referred to as the father of Jerome, and an oration delivered by the Honorable Charles H. Rutherford, U.S. Attorney.

The only thing I remember relative to the exercise was the Pledge of Allegiance to the Flag. We all stood at attention facing the Flag, hands by our sides. At a signal from our teacher, all pupils gave the Flag a military salute and all repeated together, "I pledge allegiance to my flag and to the republic for which it stands, one nation indivisible, with liberty and justice for all."

At the words, "to my flag," right hands were extended, palms up, towards the flag. They remained in that position until the end of the declaration, whereupon all hands returned to the side. Then we all sang, "America My Country, tis of Thee."

*Charles Vihel, now retired and living in Tempe, graduated from Arizona State Teachers College three years in a row. In the class of '29, he received one of the last two-year teaching certificates; in the class of '30, he received a three-year teaching certificate, and in the class of '31, he received a Bachelor of Arts degree.*

---

# Teaching at Age Fifteen

Lorenzo Rhoton

I was seven years old in 1904 when I started school in Shumway. The school building was the center of all community activities. It had a high ceiling and a stove in the center. The teacher had a recitation bench, and he would call up groups of children, for example, fourth grade math or third grade spelling, to show him what they had learned. I think I learned the most from just listening to all the other groups recite. Discipline was strict because the teacher wanted to be able to concentrate on listening to the group that was reciting instead of worrying about the behavior of the rest of the class. If one of the boys distracted the class in some way, then he would have to sit with the girls—of course this was effective punishment only up to a certain age.

I remember one workday when school was called off and the whole town came with shovels and picks and levelled off a part of the hill so we could have a basketball court. The court wasn't just for the school. The grownups wanted it too because we had a town team that played the neighboring towns.

I continued going to school in Shumway and then in Taylor. I was a good student and when it came time for me to be in high school my father wanted me to go to a bigger school than the one in Taylor so I rode a horse to Snowflake. While I was still in high school, I took the teacher exam and passed it. They needed a teacher at Silver Creek, nine miles away from my home. I got the job and started teaching on the first of September in 1913. I was two weeks short of being sixteen years old. Twenty-six children—all Mexican—were in the school, five of them older than me. I was so challenged that I probably never did a better job. The head of the school board was Mr. Bazan. Five of his children were in school so the school board always knew what was going on.

I rode my horse eighteen miles every day. One day there was a blizzard. I started out extra early because I knew it would take longer than usual, but it was still 10:00 before my horse climbed over the hill just outside the school. Mr. Bazan was waiting for me and said I must go to his house and get warm first. Actually I had to get dry. I was wearing a parka, but the snow had blown in and packed around my neck and then melted and dripped down my shirt so that I was soaked above the waist. After I was warm and dry and ready to go to school, he said "Lorenzo—the teacher must not be late for school. You will have to come and live with me." I thanked him kindly, but I was much too shy to consider his invitation seriously. I never went to the Saturday night dances either where he promised me there would be "whiskey and onions."

One day I got to school and found it closed. Over the weekend Mr. Bazan had killed a man who was trying to chop down his front door with an ax because he wanted to get to one of Mr. Bazan's daughters. Everyone in town was at the hearing to see if criminal charges would be filed. They were not, and the next day it was school as usual.

In 1914 I applied to teach in Snowflake so that I wouldn't have to make the long trip everyday. School boards did all of the hiring. I was given the job, and the first day of school when I arrived, the principal greeted me and asked if I was going to be in the eighth grade. I said "No, I am the new teacher." He swallowed hard and looked at me as though he were glad that on the first day the children only registered and went back home. Maybe by tomorrow he could figure something out.

Actually, the year turned out all right and I think he was glad I was hired. Later when I went back to earn my high school diploma, one of the boys I taught was my classmate.

There was always a kind of conflict over who was in control—the principal or the school board. Several years later I applied to be principal of the school in Show Low. In the interview with the school board I had suggested the names of some people I thought would be good teachers. I didn't get the job. I heard that in the discussion at the school board meeting, one of the members had voted against me because "That damn fool wanted to run the school."

---

*Now retired, Lorenzo Rhoton lives in Mesa and shared these memories in an interview.*

---

## UPLIFTING THOUGHTS AND DEVASTATING TESTS

Lawrence H. Kleinman

During my public school days I attended the Alma School in what was then District #4. It was a red brick building located just north of the railroad tracks on the east side of Alma School Road. This was about a mile away from home and we usually walked both ways. If there was some hurry I would ride my horse bareback. In the spring when horses shed their hair, I "haired" out pretty good. Since all pupils were to be at school at the same time and were released at the same time, there was quite a gang of us walking together, with a lot of nonsense, bickering, bantering and sometimes fist fights. It wasn't hard to start a fistfight, and my brother George started one for me on my first day at school.

I can't recall the reason, but I did not start to school at the age of six as customary, but waited a year until 1903—probably because I was so shy. Whatever it was I distinctly remember, during my first year, that I could read just as well with the textbook upside down or right side up. During the following summer, after much persistence, I began to learn to read. To try and catch up I almost drove my mother crazy having her help me, but she was patient. After learning to read I studied harder in my other subjects and succeeded fairly well.

I was considered a good speller and won many spelling matches. The best one I can remember was while in the sixth grade. They combined the fifth through eighth grades for a contest and I won on the word *business*.

Frank Dykes, principal and teacher of the seventh and eighth grades, was not as great an inspiration to me in book learning as he was in being a man, honest in every way and having courage to live up to the best that I knew.

The seventh and eighth grades met in the same room, which had much blackboard space. Each week, two of us were assigned to write a favorite saying or uplifting theme on the board where it was left undisturbed for a week. This was carried on for at least two years, and we learned many fine things thereby. My favorite was: "I hold these things to be grandly true: that a noble deed is a step toward God, lifting man from the common sod, to higher and nobler view."

In the spring of 1911, only half of the class graduated; the rest flunked. Our principal said that our final examination was sent to us from the County School Board, and that the questions were very hard. This was a new procedure and he did not think it was completely fair. Those who failed were so devastated that we held no graduation. Instead we were just given our diplomas. But Mr. Dykes told me that I was valedictorian of the class.

*Lawrence H. Kleinman, now 88 years old, lives in Mesa, Arizona where a park is named after his family.*

---

# Eighty Years in Southeastern Arizona

Irene A. Kennedy

When I first started school in 1906 at the age of six, we lived in a booming mining camp at Paradise in the Chiricahua Mountains of southeastern Arizona. It was a one-room school of all grades. Each class in turn was called to the front of the room. We sat on a bench below the blackboards to recite. The blackboards were so high that we smaller children had to stand on the bench, and then could only reach one third up the chalkboard.

Ages of the attendants ranged from six-years in the first grade to practically adult sized fifteen- to sixteen-year-olds in eighth grade. Our teacher sat at a desk on a six-inch raised platform in the front of the room. I believe we averaged thirty to thirty-five children in the class.

The larger boys carried a bucket of drinking water for about a mile as they came to school. The school was on the upper corner of the townsite. This was a donated lot, but it also was partway between the townsite and the operating copper mine a few miles up the canyon. Some families lived near the mine, and their children walked to the school as did all the rest of us. Restrooms were about fifty feet behind the school building and fifty feet apart, one for girls and one for boys. Most, but not all of the children, were Anglo.

Later in the early 1920s the schools at nearby Bonita were segregated. A family of Negroes lived at Bonita and in order for those children to attend school, a separate building was put up about one mile from the regular school. The local Mexican children and the five Negro children attended there. The Anglo children attended in the regular school building which by now had two teachers.

As far as I know, other than at Bonita, all the children in Cochise and Graham Counties attended the same schools. If black children were living in other districts, I do not know how the situation was handled. Nor do I know what arrangements the black family had when they moved from Bonita to Safford. Maybe by then the children were all past the eighth grade.

By the time I was in high school, my family had moved to California and I was going to high school in Los Angeles. However, they decided to return to Arizona, and so they sent me to Tempe. I arrived the first week of November, 1917. Dr. Matthews was the president. The school was still offering a five-year combination of schooling which would cover four years of high school and two years of college. I was placed in the third year. Some time later, the Normal School began accepting only students who had completed their first two years of high school.

After I graduated in 1920, I taught in Douglas in a school where only Mexican children attended up to the fifth grade before they went on to the regular grammar school. I taught for only a year-and-a-half because I got married. In those days a married teacher taught only in schools that were in isolated areas. I taught one year in Central, and this was the end of my teaching career until after my husband died. Then I went back to teaching and taught kindergarten for nineteen years until I retired here in Duncan.

---

*Irene Kennedy began teaching in Duncan in 1951, the year that the district's Mexican and Anglo children first began attending the same school.*

# The Last Teacher in Colter

Ida Slade Burgess

In the spring of 1918 when I was nineteen years old, I found out that high school graduates could take an exam at the county school superintendent's office and obtain a certificate to teach in Arizona. I took the examination and received my certificate. That summer I attended school in Flagstaff and was hired to teach in the Colter School District. About two weeks before school started, a dance was held at the schoolhouse and there I met the trustees and other people of the district.

On the first day of school I had fourteen pupils from first grade through seventh. It was a one-room schoolhouse with a large stove in the corner. We drew our water from a well and brought it to the school in a bucket. The children all drank from a long-handled dipper. A large bell which hung on top of the building was rung each day a half-hour before school began. This bell was later moved to the Eagar School where it was used for many years. The restrooms, of course, were outside—one for the girls and one for the boys. When the weather became cold, we found that one stove did not keep us warm. The trustees put another stove in the middle of the room. We circled our desks around it and were more comfortable.

I had two first-grade pupils. One was a little girl named Reba and the other was a bright little boy. He asked me if he could take his reading book home to show his mother and father. When he came back, he had memorized the book. I realized my mistake and had to use flash cards to teach him to read.

School was going all right when the flu epidemic hit the nation. Our school, along with all others, was closed for two months. During the time off, some of us teachers sold Liberty Bonds. We covered the two towns of Eagar and Springerville and outlying ranches on horseback. We were quite successful.

I stayed with my sister in Eagar and rode a horse to school three miles away. I wore a divided skirt and buttoned it up front and back to teach. A terrible snow storm hit our part of the country, and of course we had no snowplows. The sidewalks were impassable and everyone walked in the road where the snow was packed down. Where I had to ride, the snow was up to my horse's belly. Somehow we lived through it.

The boys who did the janitorial work had to shovel paths to the restrooms. Those buildings were not tight, so we had to take a broom with us to sweep off the seat each time we used it.

A new family moved into the district, and for about six weeks I had an eighth grader. They moved away and so did other families. At the end of the year I had only 12 pupils.

Some of the mothers planned a picnic for the last day of school. Each child brought a lunch and we had a good time. After the picnic, we went back to the schoolhouse and I gave each child a report card. I made out my reports, and my school year was over.

Not long after that I married and moved to Colorado. I may have been the last one to teach in the Colter District. Because it had so few pupils, it was disbanded and incorporated into the Eagar School District.

---

*Ida Slade Burgess taught for many years in Eagar and Round Valley and now lives in Safford.*

# Honor Roll: 1900-1919

**R. H. H. Blome**

The first "high-priced" teacher hired by the Normal School, Blome came from the University of Chicago with a Ph.D. in psychology and pedagogy. He directed the training school in Tempe until 1890 when he left to become an administrator at Northern Arizona Normal School in Flagstaff.

**Louise Boehringer**

Boehringer received her Bachelor of Science Degree in Teaching from Columbia University in 1911. In 1912, she moved to Yuma where she was elected County School Superintendent, thereby becoming the first woman to hold a public office in Arizona. She later served in the State Legislature and edited the *Arizona Teacher* and the *Arizona Parent-Teacher* magazines.

**Charles O. Case**

C. O. Case set a record in serving as State Superintendent of Public Instruction longer than anyone else. Except for the two years when Elsie Toles was in office, he served from 1912 until 1933.

**Connie and Rose Faras**

The Faras sisters, who both attended Tempe Normal, taught for a combined total of 88 years in Douglas. After their retirement, the Pirtleville School was renamed in their honor.

**Robert Lindley Long**

Long first served as Territorial Superintendent of Public Instruction in 1898. He served several more terms and also was principal of the Tempe Normal School and a member of the Board of Regents for the University of Arizona.

**Arthur John Matthews**

The first long-term president of the Normal School, Matthews came to Tempe from Prescott in 1900. During his thirty-year presidency, Arizona became a state, the Normal School became a college, and the average daily attendance of school children increased from 10,000 to 78,643.

**John Oscar Mullen**

Mullen graduated from Tempe Normal in the late 1800s and began teaching in Wickenburg when he was only 17. Between 1918 and 1948, he served as superintendent in Florence, Tempe, and Jerome.

**Andrew Christian Peterson**

After serving in the Spanish-American war, Peterson returned to his hometown to teach in the St. Johns Academy. In 1903 he went to the Thatcher Academy where he taught for two years before becoming its executive officer. He served in the Arizona Legislature and was speaker from 1919-1921. Prior to retirement, he taught at Arizona State College, Flagstaff.

**Mary Elizabeth Post**

One of the first formally educated teachers to come to Arizona, Post taught in the Yuma-Ehrenburg area from 1872-1912. Upon her retirement she received the first teacher pension granted by the State of Arizona.

# Phoenix Union High School: An Example of Modern Educational Methods

Editor's Note: *The opening of a new school was often a matter of considerable community pride as exemplified by the tone of this article condensed from Volume I of* Arizona, *July 1912. The first students attended Phoenix Union High School in the fall of 1912. The last ones in May 1982.*

The older west is dead; long live the new! Modern cities line the vanished frontier. Even the little red schoolhouse has been swept away by the besom of progress, and reared by the same untiring energy that reclaimed the desert and gave to the new State of Arizona the most advanced constitution that any state may boast, institutions of learning such as the Phoenix Union High School show what may be done by a community which is thoroughly in line with modern education methods. So where you will go there is not another school like this in the United States although presently there will be many modeled after the same plan. The ideal which has been put into execution in the building of the Phoenix Union High School, recently completed, has borrowed for its substance from the world. The architectural plan of the five great buildings that house the institution is pure Greek, chaste and beautiful; in outward appearance they might well be temples reared for the worship of Athene, the Goddess of Wisdom. And all that sincere students of education have learned about fitting the modern man or woman for a career of usefulness in the work of the world has been embodied in the curriculum which is taught in these temples of learning.

Each building contains the most modern type of washrooms and lavatories and the same building that contains the gymnasium has also perfect bathing facilities for both sexes, both pool and shower, that modern plumbing can devise. Individual lockers for the personal use of each student prevent the indiscriminate use of books, laboratory paraphernalia, gymnasium clothing, or anything through which contamination might be conveyed from one student to another. To eliminate any danger of germ infection a large number of sanitary drinking fountains are installed in each building and the unsanitary drinking cup has been entirely eliminated, the lips of the students in drinking touch nothing but the water itself.

Modern ingenuity can devise no more perfect way to ventilate a building than is used throughout the school. The open-window is out of date. Here every breath of air that enters is first filtered through water and charcoal; warmed by steam or cooled by refrigeration as required by outside temperatures, and then conducted through closed pipes to the inlets in every room. Impure air, contaminated by breathing, is constantly drawn out of the rooms and released outside the buildings, so that a constant circulation of clean, fresh air is always going forward.

Experiments have shown that one of the most potent factors making for a pupil's dullness in school work is the eye-strain resulting from too long application to printed books in insufficiently or improperly lighted buildings. Very often the eyes of children are so injured during the years of school work that they are permanently restrained from ever possessing perfect vision. In the Phoenix Union High School this condition has been guarded against and forever rendered impossible. The ideal was here a soft, diffused light in every room, without glare or shadow. And how perfectly the plans

Perspective Plan of Buildings. Phoenix Union High School.

have provided for this condition only a visit to the school can show. Here also, it might be mentioned, the older type of school desks, a perfect instrument for the growing of stoop shoulders and narrow chests have been modified in conformity with the whole plan.

The happy child whose mind is kept constantly awake and interested by something other than a dull routine of books, is the child who will most readily assimilate the knowledge of the class room. Social recreation is a most valuable and indispensible part of the modern educational ideal. To this end there has been provided not only a thoroughly equipped gymnasium, but also an auditorium with the largest seating capacity of any like structure in the city. As completed the auditorium with pit and galleries will provide seats for some fourteen hundred spectators, and there is no finer stage or proscenium in the state. It is the intention of the school management to make this auditorium not alone a meeting place for the student body but also in a sense a civic forum for the use of the whole citizenry of the city. A first class stereopticon is provided as part of the auditorium equipment.

It may be asked, "What are the purposes to be served by the great outlay necessary to build and maintain such a school?" An attempt is being made to get as far as possible from the out-worn exclusive text book method of teaching, and to substitute in its place the more modern objective and manual methods, teaching by objective training and carefully prepared lectures, which rather than detracting from the value of books, add to their service by making them understood. In addition to such studies as mathematics, languages, and the usual branches whose understanding must form a large part in the education of every man and woman, the arts and sciences here receive special attention. There is also a completely equipped department of agricultural training; domestic science and engineering courses will be opened as soon as possible. A complete course in business practice and commercial usage will also be maintained. An innovation here is in the art department where the practical work of the painter, potter, and decorator are taught, the work being done by the same methods used in commercial studios. "Learning by doing" is the keynote of the domestic science course, and the girl taking this course learns housekeeping not by the hit and miss method, which cannot be avoided in the home, but in the most scientific manner, for there is a science of the home no less than of the shop or laboratory. The homes that will be managed by Union High School girls will be homes where the problem of the high cost of living is largely solved. It has been said that there is no finer type of the modern school in the United States than this institution here in Phoenix. Before the five beautiful buildings in which the school is housed were completed, the total cost was in the neighborhood of $200,000, a cost, however, which does not even partially represent the value of the school to the community, now and in the future.

# Glimpses: 1900-1919

## DRAMATIC DAYS IN DOUGLAS
### Virginia Reed

In November of 1901 on the spot where the Gadsden Hotel would later be built, Maude Lincoln opened the first Douglas public school. The building was a 12-by-24 foot wooden structure. Besides teaching the school, which started with 19 pupils but grew rapidly, Maude Lincoln initiated the collecting of sufficient books to start a city library.

For the next year she was promised a helping teacher and offered the position of principal. But because she planned to marry Alfred C. Lockwood, she either did not, or could not, accept the position of principal. The job went to W. G. Hendrix, and the new bride organized and taught a private kindergarten in Nogales. Later she taught in public schools in Douglas, Tombstone, and Phoenix. In the 1960s, her daughter Lorna Lockwood, was Chief Justice of the Arizona Supreme Court.

By the time Mr. Hendrix took over, the school had already outgrown the little wooden shack and was meeting in the Library Hall, a building loaned by the Copper Queen Company. The 1902 fall term began with 67 students and within three months grew to 311, necessitating the hiring of three more teachers. The townspeople approved a bond of $20,000 to build a school which was completed in December of 1903. For the year-and-a-half until it was finished the five teachers continued teaching in the one-room Library Hall. Younger children came in the morning and older children in the afternoon. The furniture consisted of old desks borrowed from the Methodist Church.

With the opening of the new school, the Board elected Thomas Grindell to be principal and superintendent. He had taught at Tempe Normal School in 1897, then during the Spanish-American War had joined the Rough Riders serving under Theodore Roosevelt. After the war he returned to Arizona where for two years he was clerk of the Territorial Supreme Court. From that position, he came to Douglas where he was superintendent until May of 1905 when he joined three other men and two Mexican guides on an exploring expedition into Sonora. They intended to reach the coast of Guaymas and from there Tiburon Island in the gulf. Grindell was never seen in Douglas again.

Months later, one of the men returned in a crazed condition, unable to tell what had happened. Some think the party perished of thirst on the Sonoran desert or was held captive by Indians on Tiburon Island. The latter theory was investigated without success by the State Department.

In the emergency, Mrs. Anna Dyer was appointed principal and superintendent, serving from September 1905 until January 1906. In the history of the Douglas schools, she is the only woman to have held this position. She came to Douglas from Bisbee where she had been both teacher and principal until the Bisbee School Board informed her that she was to be replaced by a man as it was unacceptable for a woman to be principal.

*Adapted with permission from "Maude Lincoln Sets Standards," Douglas Daily Dispatch, June 23, 1966.*

## ONE BIG FAMILY IN THATCHER
### Maybell Brown Dodge

I went through school with the same group beginning in 1906 in Thatcher. We lived in town, and walked to school. It was just one big school up through the eighth grade. This allowed us to know the teachers and their families, as well as the other students. We felt like we were one big family.

We had a wood stove in the school to keep us warm. Our kindergarten teacher had us play games and build with blocks and play in the sand. I can remember her working with us, trying to make us feel comfortable at school. On the playground, the boys usually were playing baseball or shooting marbles, and the girls were playing jacks and jumping rope.

The older grades were mostly taught by men. All our teachers were stern, but nice. We had quite a bit of homework. We had to do it at night before we could go to bed.

I loved arithmetic. I remember the teacher taking rocks and having us count them and work problems with them. I think the teachers took a lot of interest in us that they don't have time to do today. We had small classes.

We went through the first eight grades, and then to the Gila Academy. All the young people from the surrounding communities came to Thatcher to attend the academy. They would rent rooms from townspeople so that they could go to school.

*Maybell Dodge now lives in California.*

## STARTING SCHOOL IN 1913
## Ilo Waggoner

We came to Arizona from Virginia in late December, 1912. We moved to a homestead in the Roosevelt School District where I grew up. Roosevelt District #66 had just been organized by the consolidation of three smaller districts. J.R. Wilson, the principal, was holding school in a tent.

Beginning in the fall of 1913 school opened in a new three-room building. However, we, who were entering the first grade, did not get to enjoy the new building. The primary grades were assigned to the Neighborhood House located across the street.

In order to understand the situation, it is necessary to remember that Roosevelt Dam began supplying irrigation water in 1913. Desert land was being leveled and placed in cultivation as rapidly as possible. Schools throughout Maricopa County were growing at a pace which required a constant supply of new buildings. At that time only real property tax payers could vote in bond elections. To the farm owners' credit, they did not hesitate to support bond issues which secured funds to build schools.

My two older brothers and I went to school (four miles) in a buggy, as did most of the students. The school provided a heavy chain, mounted on posts made of large pipe, as a place to tie the horses. This chain was located along the west side of the school ground. Near this chain were open pit toilet buildings. Drinking water was supplied by a hand pump under a gazebo-shaped shelter on one side of the cement walk leading to the building's entrance. Most of the students carried a collapsible drinking cup. Under a similar shelter on the opposite side of the walk was a porch swing.

These arrangements continued in use until about 1919, when a large building with a bell tower was completed. At that time a well was drilled near the south side of the school site. The pump was operated by a gasoline engine, and the water was stored in an overhead tank which provided sufficient gravity pressure to supply a water system. A new sanitary toilet building was located near by.

About this time, the school constructed a small building for a lunchroom. I recall hearing that this was the first hot-lunch program operated in the state. The floor in the kitchen area was about one foot higher than the floor of the dining area. The cooking was done on a large wood-burning kitchen range. The students lined up and went by the range where the food was served. The tables and benches in the eating area were made of 1" x 12" boards. This area had a dirt floor covered with about four inches of saw dust. This situation would provide a challenge for the Health Department today, but in 1919 it was acceptable, and many visitors came to observe the newly developed lunch program.

*Further memories of Ilo Waggoner are presented in the next section.*

## HIGH SCHOOL IN A PRISON
## Elizabeth H. Bennett

"School is like a prison!" rebellious schoolboys have been known to complain. But young people living in and near Yuma before the First World War welcomed the opportunity to attend high school in the Arizona Territorial Penitentiary, which had been abandoned in April of 1909 when the prisoners were transferred to Florence.

Charles Hobart, now a resident of Friendship Village, Tempe, remembers his first year of high school in the main building of the old prison. He lived on the family farm in Yuma Valley where his father used water from the Colorado River for irrigation. Overlooking the Valley from a hill west of the river was the Indian Agency; on the east side atop Prison Hill was the Territorial Penitentiary. Throughout the Yuma Valley the Colorado River meandered here and there, but between these two hills it was constricted into a narrow space thereby making the hills safe from recurring floods. Charles had a six-mile ride on horseback to reach school. During the day, the students' horses were kept with their feedbags in a shed on the prison grounds. High schools, Charles says, were a relatively new development in this pioneer area. Both his father and uncle served on local school boards. Plans were under way for a high school building, but until it was completed arrangements were made to hold school in the former prison.

The classrooms were made from what had been offices centered around the prison's dining hall. In these rooms, several teachers—both men and women—conducted classes. Charles had a man as his math teacher. His Spanish teacher was a Miss Kelly, an Anglo woman who had lived in an Hispanic neighborhood and could converse fluently with the Spanish-speaking students. There was no playing field on the Hill, but in memory of this first school, today's Yuma

High School athletic teams are called *The Criminals.*

After one year of attending school in the old prison, Charles transferred to the new Yuma High School, graduating in 1917. He then enrolled in the S.A.T.C. (Student Army Training Corps) at the University of Arizona. He later served in the Agricultural Extension Service of the University.

One of his school mates was Harry Westover whose father owned the Yuma Sun. He later became a judge and would boast, along with Charles, that he had "started his education in a prison."

*Elizabeth H. Bennett is an active member of a writers' group at Friendship Retirement Village in Tempe.*

## FROM DRILLING STUDENTS TO DRILLING TEETH
### Maud Isaacson Pace

I was born in St. Johns and was six years old in November of 1908, but my mother did not think I should go to school that year. For a short while I went to something like a kindergarten, where we spent lots of time lacing yarn into the holes punched in cardboard animals. I made several and was awarded a prize for my good work. It was a purple horse—quite large. None of us were allowed to take our prizes home until Christmas. When I went to get mine, it had disappeared. I felt bad.

When I started real school in 1909, it was held in the assembly hall, really a theater that the Whitings had built for the production of plays, musicals, and other drama events. One class was held on the stage and two others down on the main floor where the audience would sit. I do not remember moving out school desks and equipment so theater seats could be set up. Probably, they only had productions during the summer, at least in the years that the theater did double duty as a school.

Because my mother had held me out for a year, I was older and more capable than most of the first graders and so the teacher, who had sixty children in her class, put me to work patting out designs with a chalk eraser for the other children to trace around.

When school started the next year, the new St. Johns schoolhouse was finished. It was two-stories high with two large rooms upstairs and two downstairs. My most vivid memory is of the time when I was in third grade and the teacher threw a rather large book at a big overgrown boy who happened to sit at a cross-angle between me and the teacher. The boy dodged, and the book hit me just above my right eye. I saw nothing until blood poured out onto my desk. I do not remember how I got to a doctor, but I do remember going to school with my head bandaged for quite a while. The scar runs right through my eyebrow so nearly seventy-five years later I am still reminded of it whenever I use an eyebrow pencil.

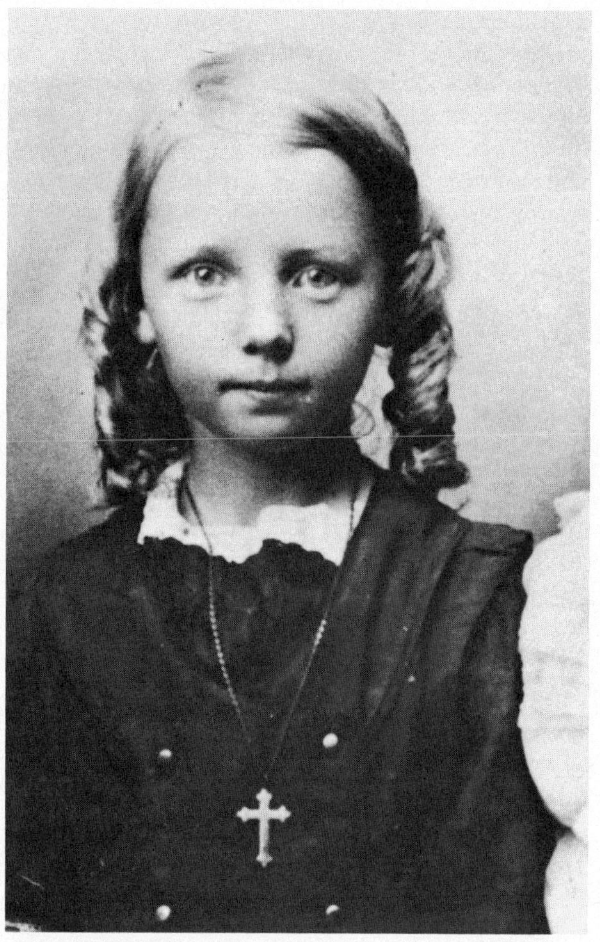

Maud Isaacson in 1911.

Years passed and eventually I returned to St. Johns to teach school in a room behind this same two-story building. By now, my former teacher had gone to dental school and was back in town with a successful dental practice. He had married my cousin and so when I had a toothache I went to him. After he finished filling my tooth, we chatted a bit and I asked him if he remembered throwing the book that hit me in the eye.

It was good that I waited until he had finished working on my tooth, because my reminder had such an effect on him. He looked as if he were going to faint.

Then he sat down and we talked some more. He told me how much he hated that year. He needed a job desperately and teaching had been the only one available. The school board agreed to pay him $65.00 a month, and then mid-year some other man came along and offered to do it for $60.00. This forced him to take the lower salary. So now he was not only frustrated with his work, but also resentful toward the school board. While he was teaching, he would look out the classroom window and envy the men he saw cleaning the irrigation ditches.

*Besides teaching in St. Johns, Maud Isaacson Pace taught in Snowflake, Heber, Salado, and Litchfield Park. She now lives in Mesa.*

## AN INTERVIEW WITH ANNIS JACKSON FLAKE
### Jennifer Peterson

During her eighty years, Annis Jackson Flake has lived all over Arizona. As a child, she lived in the small town of Pine Dale, but Pine Dale lacked a high school. Determined that she receive a diploma, Annis' parents sent her to Snowflake to board and go to school.

Annis boarded on a farm a couple of miles out of town. She called the people she stayed with "Aunt" and "Uncle." She walked to school every day. During her stay, she was expected to do household chores as well as help around the farm. One of her chores was to milk an old cow every morning and night. At first she was deathly afraid of the beast, but then she got up enough nerve to go in the barn and sit down to her task. The minute she started, the animal kicked and snorted and Annis ran from the barn to her "aunt" who gave her a white apron and told her as long as she wore it, the cow would be calm. The apron worked, and her troubles with the cow were over.

Annis attended an L.D.S. (Mormon) high school known as the Snowflake Academy. It was strict compared to our high schools today. Sixteen units (or credits) were required for graduation with a heavy emphasis on the basics. Discipline was of the utmost importance, but as in all high schools, pranks did occur. Once tobacco was placed in the school stoves. This was especially traumatic because smoking of any type was unheard of in school. Everyone knew who did it, but no one told—even after the lectures. Ditching was another "no-no," but Annis recalls ditching once when the local movie house was letting people in free if their last name began with J. Annis Jackson never could afford to go to the movies, so when she got this chance, she told her "aunt" she was going to ditch and go. At the theater, she had the misfortune of sitting in front of the principal. Needless to say, she was called in to explain herself.

Other memorable events included the installation of electric lights in the high school and her being the only girl in geometry class. Early in the 1920's, she graduated with nineteen classmates. She says the biggest difference between that era and today was that there was not as much material to work with, and extra-curricular activities were few. Libraries consisted of a shelf of books in the homeroom class, and a picnic was considered a big event.

*Jennifer Peterson was a student in Billie Cox's Mesa High School English Class when she interviewed Mrs. Flake in 1984.*

## STAYING UP FOR THE "MASQUE OF THE YELLOW MOON"
### Margaret Hurley

After I graduated from the University of California in 1912, I returned to Phoenix Union to teach English and physical education. I taught both subjects for four years, and then when the school's enrollment was large enough, I taught girls' physical education full time. One of my duties was to be in charge of all the dancing in the annual "Masque of the Yellow Moon."

The girls' dressing room was in the basement of the Old Building at Phoenix Union. Our gym outfits were full black bloomers, long black stockings, and white middy blouses. Girls wore "stays," and they didn't like to take them off for gym. Before each class I would go down the line, poking in appropriate places to make sure no one still had on her "stays." It was back to the dressing room for anyone I found still encased in whalebone.

*Margaret Hurley wrote this memory for the Pioneer Biography project of the Arizona Historical Foundation.*

Statehood parade. *Arizona Historical Foundation photo.*

## BEING STYLISH FOR STATEHOOD
### Vera McNulty Keeney

When A. J. Matthews was the head of the Prescott Schools, my brother and I were in kindergarten and first grade at the old Prescott Public School. Twelve years later I had the pleasure of renewing our acquaintance at the Tempe Normal where he was a very popular and influential college president. His financial help at Tempe is not to be forgotten. He really had a way with the legislature.

While I was at Tempe, Arizona became a state. Our group from the college had the pleasure of watching Governor Hunt and his associates march west on Washington, past the old Ford Hotel, and on to where the Statehood ceremonies were conducted.

February in Arizona can be very cold or very warm. In 1912 it chose to be hot. One persistent memory is of standing in that hot sun wearing a beautiful blue serge suit and enduring great punishment rather than unbutton one button of the modish blue jacket.

*Vera McNulty Keeney graduated from the Normal School in 1913 and is a member of the Eta Chapter of Delta Kappa Gamma.*

## THE CENTRAL SCHOOL
### Ora Webster De Concini

My parents came to Arizona from Utah in covered wagon trains in 1882. They settled first in Pima, and later in Thatcher. My mother's father and her oldest sister were among the very early school teachers in Pima where they lived in a tent for a year. But my own recollections of school begin in 1914 when I left our family farm on Webster Lane between Central and Thatcher and traveled one mile to the three-room Central school which I attended for eight years.

The school was a square cement block building with wood floors. There were outside doors to each room, and we used to line up every morning after recess and after lunch to march into school. Doors also opened between the three rooms. In back were cloak rooms for our coats. Each room had a stove for heating, and of course, there was no cooling except for whatever came through the open windows. The buildings marked "Boys" and "Girls" were about 100 feet from the school house.

In our family there were four children: Zola was the eldest, Jessie the second, Raleigh the only boy, and I,

Ora, was the youngest. Our parents were Olla Damron Webster and Oscar F. Webster. My father's brother Frank Webster with his wife Della, and seven children lived next door— actually next farm. I grew up with these seven cousins. We went to school by various means, walking, bicycles, or if there was a small child of the cousins' family, we had to hitch "Old Dick" to the buggy, and then we would all ride.

Eva Coombs Echols was my first grade teacher. When I started school, I already knew how to read, and I have only faint recollections of happenings during my first years. I do remember that I always liked to go to school, and I was upset if for some reason I had to remain home. My other teachers in the lower grades were Stella Shurtz and Elsie Jenkins. In the seventh and eighth grades, I remember Mr. Ivan Robinette (not the Phoenix lawyer) and Miss Wise, both were principals. The teachers for the lower grades were born in Central and educated at Tempe Normal School (now A.S.U.). They came back home to teach. Mr. Robinette came from elsewhere, and it was more difficult for him to have good rapport with the students and the community. I was a discipline problem for him—I was bored. First, he put my desk in front of the class so I could not whisper to neighbors. This helped little. Finally, he promoted me to the eighth grade, and I went to work and graduated at the head of the class. Finally, I was challenged.

Miss Wise was from Altoona, Pennsylvania, and I doubt that anyone in the small town knew why she came to Arizona to teach school. She rented a room with a family who lived near the school. According to rumor, she lived on shredded wheat biscuits and milk. She saved her money, and after she retired, she built a nice cement block house on the main street of Safford, just east of the business section.

Another unusual thing about Miss Wise is that she wore a black wig, done up high. It was always neat. I think that she had a better education than most of the teachers, as she tried to give us a bit of literature and other learning that we had not had before.

*Ora Webster DeConcini, the mother of Arizona Senator Dennis DeConcini, lives in Tucson.*

## COMMUTING BY BUGGY
## Lynda Dorsett

My grandmother, Nellie Raye Martin Sirrine, was one of the early graduates of the Normal School at Tempe. She became a teacher, but then she married and had children. She and my grandfather had a farm at Horne and McKillip in Mesa. Since married women were not allowed to teach in the city schools, around 1918 she commuted to work in Sacaton. Every Monday morning she would hitch two horses to the family buggy, tuck her two younger children in, kiss her eight-year-old and ten-year-old sons and her husband goodbye, and head south for twenty miles, arriving in time to open Monday morning school.

The two young children attended their mother's school. From Monday through Thursday they lived in a tent. As soon as school was out on Fridays, Grandmother would hitch up the horses and the three of them would climb in the buggy and return to Mesa so that Grandmother could do the laundry, cook the next week's food, and start the cycle all over. My father, Warren Raye Sirrine, was the eight-year-old son, and as difficult as this sounds it was not enough to discourage him from also becoming a teacher. He graduated from Arizona State Teacher's College and in the midst of the depression began teaching in a one-room school on the Arizona Strip. He went on eventually to become a superintendent in both the Yuma and the Phoenix areas.

*Lynda Dorsett did not follow the family tradition of teaching. She is a secretary in Tempe Elementary District #3.*

# 1920-1939:
# From Prosperity to Depression

The "Roaring Twenties" were in general a time of optimism, accomplishment, and prosperity. The Nineteenth Amendment gave women the right to vote, Charles Lindbergh made his triumphant solo flight across the Atlantic, and engineering feats included the building of the Holland Tunnel, the Chrysler and Empire State Buildings, Boulder (Hoover) Dam, and the Golden Gate Bridge. By the end of the decade, nearly one out of five Americans owned an automobile.

In Arizona, the most surprising education-related event of 1920 was the election of a woman Superintendent of Public Instruction. She was native-born Elsie Toles, a member of the first graduating class of Bisbee High School. She studied at Pomona College, the State Normal School at San Jose, and the University of Michigan before coming home to teach in Bisbee and Douglas. After teaching three years, she was elected Cochise County Superintendent. She described some of her experiences in an interview published in the June and September 1974 *Cochise Quarterly*. When visiting the one-room schools spread over the 6,000 square miles, she had to start each morning from her Tombstone office because there were no accommodations for staying overnight. She drove a model-T Ford and carried a five-gallon can of gas and tools for repairing both tires and engine. To get to one school perched on top of a mountain at the end of a winding road, she had to reverse her car and back up the three mile slope so the gas would feed into the carburetor.

Many of the teachers she met were untrained, ranch wives who graduated only from the eighth grade but needing the $75.00 a month studied and passed the teaching examination. Some of the homesteaders who made up the school boards were equally ill-prepared for their roles. In one confrontation a school board that wanted to fire a teacher burned the schoolhouse and announced that the teacher would now have to leave. Toles ruled in favor of the teacher, whom she considered excellent, and said that since the teacher had a contract and had violated no law the board would have to pay her salary for the rest of the year. No more schoolhouses were burned.

Her experience as County Superintendent stood Toles in good stead both when she campaigned for election and when she served as State Superintendent in 1921-22. She is credited with increasing financial support of the schools, placing the county teacher institutes under the direction of the State office, and raising and standardizing the requirements for teacher certification. She made persuasive but unsuccessful arguments that the positions of State and County Superintendents were professional roles that should be appointed, not elected. As a Republican, she was defeated in the Democratic landslide of 1922 when C. O. Case was returned to office.

When Toles was elected, there were 282 one-teacher schools scattered throughout the state. Twenty years later, consolidation of schools made possible by a greatly improved system of roads, mostly built through Public Works Administration projects, had reduced that number to 128.

Other accomplishments of the period include the founding of junior colleges. Phoenix College enrolled its first students in 1920, and in 1921 the Gila Academy at Thatcher began offering college level courses. In 1933, this Academy, which had been owned and oper-

A typical classroom, 1929.

Early 1920s class in horsemanship. *Arizona Historical Foundation photo.*

Busing in 1939.

Graduation at Phoenix Indian School, 1926. *Arizona Historical Foundation photo.*

ated by the Mormon Church since the late 1800s, was given to Graham County which has operated it ever since as Gila Junior College. The 1927 State Legislature passed an act legalizing the creation and maintenance of junior colleges and providing state funds to help operate such schools.

In the same year the two state normal schools were changed into state teachers' colleges. This was appropriate to keep up with more stringent certification requirements. Since 1921, teachers in the high school had been required to have a baccalaureate degree for regular certification. In 1936, elementary teachers were also required to earn a baccalaureate degree, while high school teachers were required to earn a master's degree or 30 graduate hours of credit. Additional boosts to professionalism came with rulings that county school superintendents must be holders of valid Arizona teaching certificates, teachers were to be included under state workmen's compensation laws, and districts must notify teachers by March 15, if they did not intend to hire them for the following year.

The 1920 federal census for Arizona showed that 56.4 percent of Arizona residents between the ages of five and twenty were attending school. By 1930, this percentage had risen to 66.8 percent. Despite a considerable decrease between 1920 and 1930 (from 15.3 percent to 10.1 percent), Arizona still had one of the highest rates of illiteracy in the nation. Illiteracy was defined as not being able to read or write one's name in one's native language. While bemoaning this fact and taking steps to improve the condition, most educational leaders attributed it to Arizona's geographical proximity to Mexico and to the existence of Indian reservations.

The relative prosperity of the 20s is reflected in the kinds of educational bills that the state legislature passed. The assumption grew that typical students were being taken care of and the state could now begin to pay attention to the atypical. In 1926, the state founded a school for female juvenile offenders, and separated the schools for the deaf and blind from the University of Arizona thereby setting the stage for state-wide expansion. In 1927, the Legislature provided funds for the establishment of a children's colony to educate the 142 Arizona children then identified as mentally defective. It also made physical education a mandatory subject in all elementary schools.

When the stock market crash of 1929 ushered in the Great Depression, Arizona schools suffered along with schools across the nation. The Depression hit rock-bottom in 1932-33, the winter that President Franklin Roosevelt held his first radio "fireside chat," that Hitler began to re-arm Germany, that the Dionne quintuplets were born in Canada, and that Congress passed the 21st Amendment repealing prohibition. On the national scene, in the fall of 1932, some 2000 rural schools failed to open and 200,000 teachers were out of work. In some poor, rural districts the Depression did not make as much difference as it did in the cities because the economy had always been a hand-to-mouth one. But no school escaped unscathed. In Arizona, state appropriations to local districts were reduced by 20 percent, repairs on buildings were postponed, no new textbooks were adopted, no supplies were provided, financial support for kindergartens was dropped, and night schools for adults were eliminated. As shown in some of the articles that follow, individuals at all levels of the educational system exercised considerable creativity as they were forced to adopt austerity measures.

Herman Elbert Hendrix was elected State Superintendent in 1933 and was the one charged with helping Arizona schools recover from the Depression. He worked with the federal government to obtain aid for the schools. He also negotiated with the Bureau of Indian Affairs for Indian children to attend public schools for which the Bureau would pay.

As the country began to recover from the Depression, the challenge was to convince poverty stricken taxpayers that "temporary" deletions made during the depression should be restored—that good schools were a necessity, not a luxury. One critic of Arizona schools in the 1930s observed that the excitment and joy had disappeared from classrooms. The center of interest had become statistics, tests, and measurements.

Superintendent Hendrix was foresighted enough to encourage going beyond this. He encouraged the re-establishment of the adult night schools and of kindergartens. He also campaigned for the teaching of environmental conservation and the use of radio and movies as educational tools.

# The Year One at Dos Cabezas

**Elizabeth Randall Crutchfield**

In May, 1922, I celebrated my eighteenth birthday. The following week I graduated from Tempe Normal School. I was ready and eager to go forth and teach the very young of Arizona.

The school's placement bureau was most capable. In early spring I was offered a position as primary teacher. The salary was $65.00 per month. I was so thankful to have an offer that I took it at once and signed a contract. A week or so later I received another offer. The pay was twenty-five dollars better. So I cancelled the first contract and signed for the second. Two more positions followed, each better pay, so I repeated my former procedure.

When I reached home, my mother, who taught in Willcox, told me there was an excellent position as primary teacher in Dos Cabezas. A friend would take me there and I could apply. Well—this was the best! One hundred and fifty dollars per month, a teacherage, cut wood for the stove and a well. I was offered the job and I accepted with no hesitation.

I came joyfully home and my family all congratulated me. Then I sat down to write and cancel my last contract.

"What are you writing about?" asked my snoopy mother. Happily I told her of my progressive good fortune. My mother was horrified! My father was horrified!

"You signed a *contract*?" said my father in a voice of dire disapproval.

"She has signed four—one after another!" said my shocked mother. "Didn't you learn anything about signing a contract to teach?"

No, I hadn't. No one at school had mentioned it.

I got a thorough scolding from my parents, but they were so happy to have me near home that they let me continue in my evil ways and take the good job at Dos Cabezas.

It was a memorable year. I lived in the four-room teacherage with my principal, Mamie, and her four-year-old daughter, Margaret. I assured my parents that I was well chaperoned by this older woman. Later I discovered that this "older" woman was only twenty-eight.

Dos Cabezas was a very small town at the foot of Dos Cabezas peaks, two miles below the mine. The peaks were called Dos Cabezas because they resembled two heads side by side. Families of the miners lived around us. Ranches were spread throughout the valley and the children rode in to school.

I had first, second, and third grades. Blanche had the fourth, fifth, and sixth grades. Mamie was principal and taught seventh and eighth grades. I had thirty-five children. The ages ranged from Mamie's daughter Margaret, aged four, to José, who was sixteen and also in first grade. Fortunately I had attended a country school all through the elementary grades, and did my practice teaching in a rural school out in the valley.

Four-year-old Margaret learned to read very well during the first month of school. All the children loved her, so she was a great help tutoring the other first graders.

José was not an eager student. To sit with all those little people was a great humiliation. Also, his father kept him out to help work as a section hand on the railroad whenever he needed him. But the rest of the time the father insisted he come to school. So José played hooky a good bit of the time.

I sent word home to the father about the hooky, so he gave poor José a few swats. One morning the children came to me with word that José had come to school but had climbed down the stone-lined well. I went and looked down. There he stood ten feet down, a foot on either side. I just left him. I figured he'd finally get tired and come up. I hoped he wouldn't get tired and fall in. He finally came up and into the classroom. I didn't say anything. But I wrote a note to his father telling him if he wanted José to learn anything, he'd better not take him out to work.

Mr. Martinez came to school bringing poor José with him telling me I should whip José.

"No, no Mr. Martinez," I protested. "I don't need to do that."

"Yes," insisted Mr. Martinez.

He made José lean over with his hands on his knees. I gave him two or three whacks with the yardstick. He howled loudly and then went home with his father. He never missed another day of school. And he learned to read quite well.

The county school superintendent was a great lady. She came by every so often with the county nurse to see how things were going. She had a motto which I always remembered during the thirty-five years I taught school. "To be a good teacher, you must make friends in three places. You make friends with the children, make friends with their parents, and make friends with the teachers you work with."

The nurse always examined heads for lice and she always found them. She had a simple recipe for getting rid of lice. Everyone lined up in the back yard of the school house. Then they rubbed their heads with kerosene. We kept a supply of rags at school. We wrapped the heads in a turban, pinned it with a safety pin and then sent the kids home. They kept the rag on for a couple of days. Then they had to wash their heads with hot water and vinegar and lots of soap. This would eliminate lice for a couple of months. Then we repeated the treatment. Some mamas protested. But Mamie, who was small and blond and mighty, settled the problem very quickly.

I had an evening class of a dozen or so miners from up on the hill. They were studying to take their citizenship exams. We met twice a week all year and they really worked at it.

We had a Nativity Play at Christmas. Everyone came from miles around and they all brought food for a great Christmas dinner.

Mamie lived in Bisbee where her husband was a miner. She went home every weekend and sometimes she took me. It was fun. Other weekends I had to hunt around for a ride into Willcox, where my family lived. There was a very kind man and his wife who, for the first part of the year, drove down the valley through Willcox every Friday. His truck was loaded with bags full of something and a tarp was fastened over all. It turned out that he had a still up in the valley beyond Willcox. He and his wife got arrested, and I had to hunt for another ride.

We had dances and food sales to raise money to buy a phonograph for the school. We finally got it. We sang in Mamie's room twice a week. She played the piano. My job was to conduct physical education. We had races, broad and high jumps, and baseball.

Finishing the year in a blaze of excitement, two girls in the eighth grade graduating class married two miners from my night school. According to custom, each bride received $50.00 from the groom. This was for the trousseau. So Mamie and I were asked to take the money to Bisbee and get the girls' bridal clothes. This may be hard to believe, but for the $50.00 each girl got a white dress and veil, another dress, shoes, hose, nightie, and underwear. It was fun and the girls were ecstatic.

The double wedding was held the morning after school closed. The priest came from Bisbee. The brides (age 15) were lovely. A huge wedding breakfast followed. Then everybody danced all afternoon. There was a big dinner at night, dancing all night, and still going strong the next morning. But Mamie and Margaret and I loaded up and went home. We were exhausted.

Twenty years later I went home to Willcox for my father's funeral. We were sitting together by the fire after the service when there was a knock at the door. When I opened it there was José Martinez and his wife who had been one of our Dos Cabezas girls. They were dressed in their best and shook hands and offered their condolences. José was now head of the section in Willcox. He had a promising family of eleven children, all doing well. I had not seen him or his wife since Dos Cabezas. The county school superintendent, Helen Kieling, was right about making friends.

---

*Elizabeth Randall Crutchfield is now retired and living in Glendale.*

# The Neebs of Neeb Hall

Rayma Bachman Neeb

I was born and raised in Minnesota and graduated from Mankato Normal School, now a branch of the University of Minnesota. In 1927, I migrated to California to attend UCLA, but shortly after arriving there I was offered a position to teach "auditorium" at Emerson Elementary School in Phoenix. I enjoyed the job of being a public speaking teacher. The students discussed current events, gave speeches and readings, and produced plays. But four years later when I married Lewis S. Neeb, I was forced to resign since married teachers were not acceptable.

In 1938, I was given the position of Executive Secretary of the State Board of Technical Registration for Engineers and Architects for the State of Arizona. The first year we had only ten applicants. The office was in our home, but as the population grew so did the number of applicants and an office was opened in Phoenix. One of the most notable I helped register was Frank Lloyd Wright.

I am now 82-years-old, and wherever I go in the state someone comes up to tell me they were one of my husband's students. Just recently when I went to my granddaughter's wedding in Yuma, a man came up to tell me that he was working with my husband back in the 1930s building solar water heaters very similar to the ones being built today.

My husband's students affectionately called him *maestro*, but everyone else called him L.S. He was born and raised in Cincinnati where he graduated from the high school in which his mother taught German and Latin. After high school, he attended and graduated from what is now Bradley University. He came out west to teach and coach athletics in Reno, Nevada. When World War I broke out, he and his football team tried to enlist in the army. They took the boys but rejected him because he wore glasses.

He went to work in the Navy shipyard in Vallejo, California. While there he designed a gear to be used in the building of ships. It was patented, and in a patriotic gesture, he gave the patent to the United States Government.

In 1917 he came to Tempe to teach manual arts and coach athletics at Tempe Union High School. Under his leadership, Tempe High won the state championship in baseball. Those team members who are living still reminisce about the championship and about the time they were called on to help capture a fugitive prisoner who had escaped from Florence and was hiding behind the Tempe Butte.

In those days Arizona was a small state, at least in regards to population, and when anything happened everyone was called on to help. The first governor of Arizona, George W. P. Hunt, was my husband's fishing pal.

From Tempe, L.S. went to Bisbee to organize a vocational school in cooperation with the Phelps Dodge Company and the Bisbee Public Schools. During this time he also studied for advanced degrees in education and engineering at the University of Arizona and the University of Southern California.

After leaving Bisbee he taught in the Engineering Department of Phoenix Junior College and also coached basketball. Few students had cars and so he not only coached the team but took his boys home after practice. One of his students was Clarkson Ogelsby. Clarkson dropped out of school, but my husband went to his home and persuaded him to return. It was a fortunate change of mind because he went on to become Head of the Department of Engineering at Stanford University and is known as the father of the modern freeway system.

Another student that he later befriended was Emerson Harvey, the first black to play football for Arizona State College. Harvey went on to become a highly respected teacher in the Phoenix Elementary District.

In 1931, Dr. Ralph Swetman hired L.S. to be Head of the Department of Industrial Arts at Arizona State College. There were fewer than 1,000 students, and Tempe was a city of 1,500. L.S.' salary was $3,000. He asked permission to expand the scope of the department to include technology. He then hired James Elmore and Melvin Ensign to teach beginning classes in architecture. He also hired George Ross and Charles Merritt to teach beginning engineering classes. These were the seeds from which the present Colleges of Architecture and Engineering grew. It was because of my husband's part in establishing these colleges that Neeb Hall on the ASU campus was named for him.

In 1934, L.S. went to the City Council of Tempe and asked permission to build and put up a star on the Butte during the Christmas season. The first star was made by the students with no cost to the city. Three years later, he asked permission to add camels—here again, they were built by the students.

---

*Rayma Bachman Neeb lives in Tempe.*

---

## THE ENGINEER MEETS THE TEACHER

Thomas Diehl

In the late thirties, Mr. Harrison Lavender was Vice President and General Manager of the Western Mining Operations of the Phelps Dodge Corporation. Mr. Lavender prided himself on being a rough, tough mining engineer. On one of his trips to Ajo, he asked the Manager of the New Cornelia Branch, Mike Curley, if there was a teacher in the Ajo schools named Amanda Pederson. Mike Curley reported that there was indeed a Miss Pederson teaching in the Ajo High School. Mr. Lavender asked that he be taken to the school to see this teacher.

When Mr. Lavender, Mr. Curley, and the superintendent of schools were on their way to Miss Pederson's classroom, Mr. Lavender told the other two to keep quiet. He would do all the talking. The three arrived in Miss Pederson's room just a minute or two before the end of the period. Miss Pederson was a very dignified and business-like person and she did not appreciate interruptions. She looked at the visitors, finished her instructions to the students, and dismissed them. Miss Pederson looked at the visitors again with a well-what-do-you-want? expression.

Harrison Lavender said, "Hi, Amanda." No one ever called her "Amanda." She was always addressed as "Miss Pederson." He then said, "You don't remember me, do you Amanda?"

Miss Pederson just stared at him and shook her head. He continued, "Who was the worst behaved boy in your class when you were going to grade school in Yankton, South Dakota?"

Without any hesitation, Miss Pederson pointed her finger at him and said, "You are Harry Lavender."

*Thomas Diehl, a long time resident of Ajo, says this is a widely told story of school and community relationships.*

---

# A Year in the Sun

Mabel Frederick Evans

My dad worked for the Santa Fe Railroad, and having heard good reports about the Arizona schools he bid on a job near Phoenix. In February of 1928 when I was eleven years old and in the sixth grade, we moved from northern New Mexico to Peoria, Arizona. The whole experience was unforgettable. We went from winter to what we thought was surely summer. I also had my first encounter with segregation, which I could not understand. In our small New Mexico town the population was largely Hispanic (the preferred term at that time was *Spanish-American*) and there were no blacks. I would guess that in my classroom of thirty or thirty-five pupils, there were no more than a half-dozen Anglos. My best friend was Hispanic. I recall no awareness of any differences in our names or backgrounds. We were just "best friends." So it was puzzling to me to see all the Hispanics plus the blacks gathering to attend their own school across the street from the house we had rented. Their building was old and quite large. The new school for Anglos in grades five and six was about eight blocks away with few rooms but each one was spacious with many windows. It was across the road from the high school. To further confuse me, Spanish speaking Luis and Maria from Puerto Rico were in my class, and they were friendly and well-liked. Why were they not attending school in the large gray building down the street? I cannot say.

School had always been enjoyable for me, but never, except in Peoria did I not look forward to weekends! The end of the spring term and the beginning of summer vacation saddened me to the point of tears! The reason was my teacher, Miss Floy Hawkins, from Phoenix. Teachers before her I had liked, but Miss Hawkins I loved. She set high standards, both in conduct and studies, and we tried very hard not to let her down. She encouraged, sympathized, or chastised—all the while making us feel that she really cared about us.

The spring term ended and real summer arrived. Those school extollers must have forgotten to tell my Dad about summers. But in spite of the heat and the bugs—species we never even knew existed—summer held for me many wondrous things. I loved going barefoot, but would walk only where there was shade.

In New Mexico we lived upstairs in the railroad depot. Our yard was coarse gravel and no trees, but here in Peoria we had a real house with grass. There were trees we could use for climbing and for picking apricots, peaches, oranges, lemons, and grapefruit. It seemed heavenly to sit in the swing under the grape arbor and reach up to pick whichever kind of grape we wanted. We climbed fig trees and ate figs until our mouths and throats felt raw, and when the milky tree sap got on us we itched all over. Doodlebug holes in the sand intrigued us. When we laid down and blew into them, the sand would fly out and we could find the little doodlebug.

In spite of how much I liked the summer, my parents were ready to retreat back to the cooler mountains of New Mexico. Dad bid on the first suitable job that came along, and in December he got it. In the meantime I had started back to school and was fortunate that someone had decided to keep at least one room of seventh graders in the smaller building rather than sending us over to the high school. Most important, Miss Hawkins remained my teacher. I went to the high school building for music and sewing. In sewing I got one six-weeks grade of AA++ called double A double plus, my only experience with such a lofty grade. In the high school cafeteria I was introduced to one of life's special pleasures, the recently invented chocolate-covered ice cream bar tightly wrapped in silver foil—an "Eskimo Pie." It cost a nickel.

Shortly after Christmas my Dad left for his new job. Partly for the sake of our education and partly to assuage my sorrow at leaving, it was agreed that my mother would stay so that we children could finish the school year. But it was not to be. Just weeks after Dad left, an epidemic of spinal meningitis broke out. It struck the mothers with the same kind of fear and panic that my generation of mothers experienced when we heard the word *polio* or *infantile paralysis*. For a short while we would hear rumors at school and among friends. This one or that one had caught the disease and was hovering near death or was paralyzed or both. Each morning another empty desk—or two—or three stared at us. Parents were keeping their children home. Soon all the schools were closed indefinitely.

My parents were understandably very nervous as they had lost my little brother to some form of meningitis only a few years before. It was not long before they made the decision that we should return to New Mexico immediately. Mother arranged for me to meet Miss Hawkins at school. When I had finished gathering my things up and was ready to leave, we hugged each other and said a tearful goodbye. It was a sad day for me. I never saw Miss Hawkins again, but I have felt her influence all through my life.

From that special year of Arizona spaciousness, I went back to living upstairs over the train depot on an Indian reservation and attending a school where all eight grades met in one room. That too was interesting, but very different from Arizona.

---

*Although Mabel Frederick Evans now lives in El Paso, Texas, she did return to Arizona in the 1950s where a son graduated from Nogales High School. She now has a daughter attending ASU.*

---

## THE AROMA OF VEGETABLE SOUP

Alice Arguijo Jones

In the early 1930s I attended the Seventh Street School in Douglas. Joseph Jones, the man who became my husband, was also a student there, as was former Governor Raul Castro. However, Governor Castro attended a few years before we did. We were there during the Great Depression. It was an elementary school, grades one through six. The Principal, Sarah Marley, who was strict but kind, would daily oversee the cooking of vegetable soup for the entire school population. The aroma of that soup was heavenly as all morning it wafted down the hallways and through the classrooms.

Many children had not had a substantial breakfast, if any, and so were hungry. Miss Marley's "soup line" was a tremendous act of kindness and generosity which stands out in my childhood memories. I have heard that the name of the school was later changed so that it is now fittingly known as Sarah Marley Elementary School.

*Alice and Joseph Jones now live in Harbor City, California.*

---

# Four Years for the Price of Two

**Joel Benedict**

I have been involved in various kinds of teaching ever since 1930—that's more than fifty years—but the accomplishment I am the proudest of occurred early in my career in the midst of the depression. I went to the little town of Mayer up in Yavapai County to be principal of the school. There were four teachers including me. I was getting, I think, $175.00 a month. That was a lot of money. In my first job in Gilbert my salary had been $140.00 a month. The total Mayer budget for a year of school was only a little over $8,000. Of course the biggest part of this went for teachers' salaries. The next biggest expense was for coal to heat the building, then the janitor received $200.00 a year, and there were miscellaneous expenses for supplies, and such.

As modest as this budget was, it was hard for the town to meet it. There was just no money. Even the county treasury didn't have money. Some months we teachers got our pay in small checks called warrants which came in ten and fifteen dollar amounts. We could take them around to pay our bills, one at the grocery store, another at the gas station, and still others to pay the rent, etc. Creditors had no choice but to take them and wait until the county treasury had enough money to give cash for the warrants.

Actually the people in town were happy to take the warrants because they had so few chances to get money. The only people in the whole town who were on a payroll—who had any regular salary—were the four teachers and three or four section hands on the railroad. Everyone else just had to make do.

Mayer was basically a mining town but during the depression the mines were closed. Some people farmed a little or raised a few cattle around Big Bug Creek, and a few scratched a little money out of the ground. It's placer mining country and ambitious parents used to go out on Big Bug Creek on a weekend. They would go as a group, have a picnic, and pan for gold usually getting enough to buy shoes for the kids so they could go to school.

The school was an elementary school, but it had ten grades. I could find no record of who started it that way, which is one of the reasons that I did some writing while there to record a bit of history. As far as I knew, no one had ever gone on to college from the Mayer school. To go on to high school was a challenge. People had to find a relative or someone living in Prescott nearly fifty miles away who would be willing to board a student while they went to high school. But during the depression families couldn't afford to pay for this or for the transportation, so there was no way for Mayer students to finish high school.

When I arrived, two students had just graduated from the tenth grade and were anxious to go on. Finding some way for them to do this was my first priority. I had gone to high school in Camp Verde and remembered my principal as a man of wide experience with good ideas. He was now principal in Payson, and so I went for a visit to see if he had any ideas. He suggested that we have a leap-frog system. "You still stay with your two years," he said, "but you teach the ninth and eleventh grade one year and the tenth and twelfth the next."

This seemed like a good idea and I set out to make plans. I went to Tucson and got the plan approved by O.K. Garretson, who was the State High School Visitor. I didn't change any of the teaching staff or try to hire new teachers, but I did ask some of the teachers who taught in lower grades and got out a little early to teach maybe an English class or something like that. The first year, they were teaching Latin as a foreign language. I changed that immediately to Spanish because I couldn't teach Latin. I didn't know much about Spanish, but as soon as I knew I had the contract for the Mayer job I went up to Flagstaff and took a course in Spanish.

But now that I had the plans made, I still had to sell them to the community. I put together a 30-page booklet that I called an annual report. I started out with a map of the school district showing the legal boundaries, the school schedule, a directory of the school board members, the teachers' names and subjects, and the projected enrollments and budgets for the next three years. I went to the county office and got the budgets, and cost per pupil for every school in the county and also in the state so that people could see where we stood and could compare our costs with our ability to pay. In Yavapai County the costs per child for 1931-32 ranged from $62.22 in Camp Verde where average daily attendance was 107 students to $214.25 at Crown King where the average daily attendance was only nine students. I also showed in the report how our students ranked on the Stanford Achievement Test, and I listed the requirements for high school graduation and university admission. As part of all this, I mentioned the possibility of adding two more years to our school. The projected budgets showed that it would not cost any more, at least in the first couple of years. But still I was worried that depression-poor voters would not want to take the risk of making changes in the structure of their school.

I made enough copies of the report for every taxpayer in town. I sent them out and then personally called on each family with a petition to establish a high school. I got only one turndown. I don't remember how many taxpayers there were, but I still consider getting this level of support for the high school my greatest accomplishment. The plan went into operation the next year, and I was genuinely proud when we had our first high school commencement.

John R. Murdock was Dean at the Tempe Normal School and he travelled to Mayer at his own cost to give the commencement address. One of the girls who graduated wanted to go on to college, but had practically no chance. He promised her a job if she could come to Tempe. I helped her get $50.00 to pay registration fees, and she worked for him all through college. Later when he went to Congress in Washington, D.C. he took her with him as a secretary, and then she took her younger sister back and put her through school. From Mayer, Arizona to Washington, D.C. was a long ways, but that's how people helped each other out.

For being such a small school, we provided a surprisingly good academic program. High school students were required to have four years of English and I think three years of history. They had to have general science and then either biology, chemistry, or physics. We couldn't possibly get equipped for chemistry or physics so we took biology and more biology. In the country like that, it was easy to find specimens.

There was no space for things like shop and industrial arts, but I've always done lots of building of things and I would involve students whenever I could. One activity we had was the making of a yearbook, all in-house except for the trimming and binding. The books ended up costing each student only about $1.50, and so everyone bought one.

When I first went to Mayer the school didn't even own a ditto machine, so I bought a little portable and paid for it myself. The school didn't have a typewriter either. I took mine in to be used both for school business and for students to learn typing. When we wanted to do a yearbook, I talked with Fred Steiner from the Peterson, Brooke, Steiner and Wist Company in Phoenix. He gave me some hints on doing a dittoed yearbook and putting the pictures in with blueprint paper. This meant it could all be done right in school. It was a very simple thing, but quite effective. My copies of these yearbooks are now over 50 years old, and they're still in good condition.

An uncle of mine had a postcard size camera. He planned to have a hobby of taking pictures and learning to develop his own. He never did get around to doing any developing, but we made good use of his camera. The negatives were the perfect size from which to make our pictures. We would put a printing frame around the negative, hold it to the blueprint paper, run out into the sun for a three minutes exposure, and then bring it back as a picture page ready to be inserted in someone's yearbook. Since each page had to be done separately, it's lucky we weren't making 500 copies.

Something else special that we had were motion pictures. There was no movie house or any entertainment in town except for a pool hall. The PBSW company helped us to get into the movie business. That company has a history of its own that deserves to be included in a history of Arizona education. The partners: Ralph Peterson, Hilliard Brooke, Frederick Steiner, and Martin Wist, all met at the end of World War I at Fort Whipple. They had all contracted tuberculosis during the war and needed to live in Arizona. They opened a shop in Prescott for gift cards and books, and then they decided to come to Phoenix and open up PBSW. They always looked for ways to help out schools and in turn get school business. Martin Wist met a fellow who had a whole bunch of sixteen millimeter entertainment films. This man talked Wist into stocking these films in their store as incentive to sell projectors to small communities like ours. The idea was that if we bought the projector, we could show the films and gradually pay for the projector with the profits from charging people 10 cents to see the movies.

This worked out fine for the townspeople in Mayer as well as for the school. Once we had the projector, then we could show educational films in nearly every subject matter. People have asked me if this is where I first developed my interest in film and audio-visual education. This experience in Mayer helped, but I first got interested when I started college in 1926. My folks gave me $25.00 and from there I had to make it on my own. I was a janitor around town for 25 cents an hour, but I also had an extra job that I liked more. I was the relief operator for the theater, the one by the Phoenix city hall that was just torn down in 1984. They were silent films and I only got paid on the nights when the regular operator didn't work. But I could always see the movie for free.

I worked with the boys' basketball team and the scout troop. We made several trips in my Model-T Ford. It was fairly easy to gather up some food and a bedroll for each boy. When we would come to Phoenix we would stay at the Scout Pueblo. We didn't have to come just for scout events, we could come anytime and sleep there as long as we had our own food and equipment. It was a big outdoor adventure. There was an Indian caretaker that the boys really liked. He died about five ago when he was ninety years old. He used to tell the kids stories and teach them Indian dancing.

If we were going on basketball trips we did much the same. Of course basketball was played in the daytime, but supposing you went from Mayer to Payson, you had to stay overnight and so you would take a bedroll. The girls basketball team mostly made shorter trips. But I think they did go to Payson a time or two. We would write the principal of the school and he would arrange for the girls to stay with families.

About the only visitor we ever had at school was the county school superintendent. I don't know how often he came and I was never sure just what his duties were. I suppose he was supposed to supervise us and maybe offer a bit of training. He would usually take over the class and give a demonstration lesson, which I think was also a way of testing the children. We didn't have many exams or standardized tests, but we all got prepared for the county superintendent's visit.

He could never make a surprise visit because Prescott was fifty miles away and someone would always let us know he was on the way. We had some famous county superintendents; you could find interesting stories about some of them. While I was the principal in Mayer we had a superintendent who was an odd kind of fellow, rather aggressive. He bought himself an airplane. This was the barnstorming days when they had those old fashioned planes. He flew over to Oak Creek where there were several one-room schools and not enough children—he thought—to continue the expense of separate schools. His intention was to lapse the district. He went to see the school board to close a school and one of those old ranchers backed him up against a barbed wire fence and told him he wasn't going to lapse that district, and he didn't.

---

*Joel Benedict is now professor emeritus at ASU and is still producing educational media.*

# Honor Roll: 1920-1939

**Joel A. Benedict**

Benedict began teaching in Arizona schools at the beginning of the depression. He later founded the Audio Visual Education program at Arizona State University and the Central Arizona Film Cooperative. In 1962-63, he established an Audio Visual Center for the Eastern Region of Nigeria.

**Mary C. Bons**

First elected to the Phoenix Union High School Board in 1933, Bons served for the next 30 years. She received an Award of Merit from the National Vocational Association in honor of promoting work-related education.

**Eulalia "Sister" Bourne**

Shortly after statehood Bourne began teaching in one-room schools on southern Arizona ranches. She recounted her nearly fifty years of teaching in two highly acclaimed books, *Nine Months Is a Year at Baboquivari School* (1968) and *Ranch Teacher* (1974), published by the U of A press.

**Mary A. Brown**

First elected in 1933, Brown served as Navajo County School Superintendent for 22½ years.

**Marjorie Entz**

In 1924 Entz graduated from Mesa High School, went away to college, and then returned to teach physical education for 36 years. She founded and directed the well-known Rabbettes marching and rope twirling group.

**Grady Gammage**

Gammage had already distinguished himself as a student at the University of Arizona, as superintendent of schools in Winslow, and as president of the Normal School in Flagstaff when he was chosen in 1933 to become president of Arizona State Teachers College. In a two-stage campaign, he changed a teachers college into a multi-purpose university.

**O. K. Garretson**

O. K. Garretson served as the high school inspector for the North Central Accreditation Team. He later became Dean of the College of Education at the University of Arizona.

**C. L. Harkins**

Harkins began teaching in a one-room school in Apache County in 1931. He served as school principal (Cochise and Yuma Counties), local superintendent (Madison Elementary District), county superintendent (Yuma), member of the State Board of Education, and State Superintendent of Public Instruction.

**Herman E. Hendrix**

The first person with a doctorate to be elected State Superintendent of Public Instruction (1933-41), Hendrix came to Arizona in 1917 to become superintendent in Miami. He later served on the faculty of Northern Arizona Normal School and was superintendent in Mesa.

**Veora Johnson**

Johnson began teaching at Booker T. Washington school in Mesa in 1927. She became principal in 1945 and as such was the first black educator in the city to hold an administrative post.

**Harvey McKemy**

McKemy became superintendent of Tempe School District #3 in 1934 and served in that capacity for nearly three decades. In the beginning years, McKemy also served as principal of one of the two Tempe schools and arranged for hundreds of college students to do their student teaching.

**Emery W. Montgomery**

Montgomery came from Bedford, Indiana to Phoenix in 1925 to assume the principalship of Phoenix Union High School and Phoenix College. When he retired from the district superintendency in 1953, there were five high schools, plus the college, with several more soon to be built.

**Winona E. Montgomery**

In the 1920s, Montgomery began a 40-year teaching career at Phoenix Union High School. She was a leader in teacher organization and in recruiting excellent students to become teachers.

**Ira D. Payne**

The Payne Building on the ASU campus is named for this young Stanford graduate who in 1911 came to be in charge of the training school and stayed until 1953. In the 1920s, he was the one who encouraged and pushed for the change in status from a normal school to a teachers' college.

**Cordelia M. Perkins**

From 1927 through 1955 (except for the war years), thousands of Phoenix high school students participated in the Masque of the the Yellow Moon Pageant usually directed by Perkins. In a history of the Phoenix Union High School System, she was described as "a female counterpart of P. T. Barnum or Bill Cody, with a dash of Cecil B. DeMille and a sprinkling of Flo Ziegfield."

**Ralph W. Swetman**

When Swetman came to be president of Arizona State Teachers College in 1930, he not only had the depression to contend with but also the challenge of obtaining accreditation. This necessitated more than a 50% turnover in faculty because all academic area teachers had to have a master's or doctor's degree.

**Harvey L. Taylor**

From 1927-33, Taylor was president of Gila Junior College. he left to serve for the next 20 years as superintendent of Mesa Union High School where he was active in professional organizations and founder of the Arizona Association of Student Councils.

**Flora M. Thew**

When Thew School in Tempe was named in 1958, Thew was the longest continuously employed Arizona classroom teacher. People in Tempe still say that she never had a first-grader who didn't learn to read.

**Elsie Toles**

In the same year that the Nineteenth Amendment gave women the right to vote, Cochise County Superintendent of Schools Toles surprised many people by being elected State Superintendent of Public Instruction.

**Charles Ilo Waggoner**

Waggoner began teaching in the Washington District in 1929. He later served as an assistant to Ed Ring, Maricopa County Superintendent, and then went on to become Superintendent of the Kyrene District where in the 1960s he helped establish the first on-site training program for ASU education students.

# Mixing Whiskey and Education

Glenn S. Pace

In such small Mormon Communities as Snowflake, Taylor, St. Johns, Joseph City, Shumway, and Woodruff, prohibition did not make a lot of difference. Alcohol was forbidden by the teachings of the Church, so anyone who drank had to do it secretly. There were no public bars, and the chief non-church entertainment consisted of dances at various schoolhouses. The floors would be waxed with chips of candles, an orchestra would play, and everyone from miles around—both Mormon and non-Mormon—would come.

There were usually some people who brought whiskey, but it would have been unthinkable to bring it inside the schoolhouse. Instead they would hide it in nearby bushes or trees so they could slip out for occasional drinks. It was a common practice for teenage boys when they approached a school dance to pick up a handful of sand from an ant bed, give it a fling, and then listen for where it would tinkle against glass. If they had a good ear and didn't mind sticking a hand into a dark bush that might have a snake in it, they could get a free swig of someone's whiskey.

But the story I'm going to tell about mixing whiskey and education took place in broad daylight. The forty or so kids who went to Woodruff Elementary School in 1925 probably can't remember any of the specific facts they learned that year, but they can remember the day the teacher had a fight. A man came to school and began an agitated conversation with the teacher, who happened to be my older sister's new husband. This was his first teaching job, and they were living as part of our large family. I was eighteen years old so I wasn't in school, but I heard so many accounts of the fight that I feel like a witness.

The teacher sent the students out to recess so they wouldn't hear the conversation. If he had realized what was going to happen, he probably would have kept everyone inside and just excused himself. The students, who obediently went outside, were soon joined by the two men in a terrible scuffle. As soon as they got clear from the school door, they really started fighting. The man's children were in the school and so were my younger brothers and sisters, but no one joined in or called out moral support. They were too frightened. The man was bigger than the teacher but he was also older, and the teacher was filled with the fury of a man unjustly accused—of what, no one knew.

Eventually the teacher got the man down and pinned him to the ground. He sat on his stomach, held his arms with one hand, and with the other rubbed and slapped the man's bloody nose demanding that the man promise to go home and keep his mouth shut.

The man must have promised because the teacher let him get up and limp out of the school yard. The teacher went back in, cleaned himself up, and rang the bell for class to resume. Although everyone in town discussed the fight, as far as I know, no one asked either the teacher or the man for an explanation, and they did not offer one.

It was five years before various townspeople provided me with enough bits and pieces that I could figure out what happened and realize that I had unknowingly played a key role in the matter. In small towns the custom was for men teachers to also serve as the scout master. My brother-in-law willingly agreed to this and was determined to do a good job of it. The boys wanted to make a trip to the Grand Canyon and so they were trying to earn some money. The most successful, but also the most difficult of their projects, was to go out in the hills and gather wood from the cedar trees. They would chop the small and gnarled branches

Woodruff in the 1920s.

into stove-sized pieces and make the straight lengths into fence posts. At last they had a wagon load to take to Holbrook to sell.

Two of the older boys were chosen to make the trip. They went five miles on the dirt road that leads from Woodruff out to Highway 77 running between Snowflake and Holbrook. Then they had to go eight more miles on this highway. The road surface was too hard on the horses' feet so they moved off the highway and walked alongside it. From this angle, one of them noticed a box hidden in a culvert under the highway. When they looked inside, they found Mason jars filled with bootleg whiskey.

They left it where it was but coming back home that night when they checked the culvert and found it still there, they loaded it into the empty wagon and brought it to my scoutmaster brother-in-law. When my mother learned what was in the box, she wouldn't let it inside her house, not because prohibition made whiskey illegal but because the Mormon "Word of Wisdom" made it a sin. She told him to hide it in the granery, then never to touch it again, but to notify the sheriff to come and get it.

I listened with interest to this conversation because the former deputy sheriff in Woodruff had told me that when whiskey was confiscated and the bottles were broken, it wasn't really whiskey but only weak tea that spilled out and soaked into the ground. In a community as poor as Woodruff, it went against the grain to waste something so valuable. He told me it was given to the town nurse-midwife to use "for medicinal purposes," but I suspected that she received only a small portion of what was taken in.

It was my job to milk and feed the cows, and so when I went to the kitchen for the milk bucket I put a few mason jars and some water in the bucket and went on down to the barn. I figured that as long as the sheriff was going to dilute the whiskey with 90 percent tea, I might as well help out a bit. I filled my jars with the whiskey taking half from each and refilling them with water. It looked and smelled pretty much the same. I took my jars out and hid them in the hollow centers of two or three corn shocks standing in the field. Although I didn't drink, I knew men in town who did, and at Christmas time I distributed some welcome gifts. No one asked where they came from, and I doubt that anyone connected them to the school teacher's fight a couple of months earlier. Certainly I didn't.

What had happened was that as people heard about what the scouts had found they came to my brother-in-law and made discreet inquiries. The angry man who came to school had given a large donation to the scout troop—as much as the boys could have earned with three or four wagon-loads of wood. In exchange for this donation, the scoutmaster had let the man know where the treasure was hidden. When it disappeared from the granery, I assumed the sheriff had taken it. Instead, it was this man, who felt cheated when it turned out to be half water.

In 1978, Woodruff had a centennial party to celebrate its founding. When people began reminiscing, someone brought up the school teacher's fight, and I confessed the part I had played in it. No one was more surprised than were the man's children who had wondered for fifty years why their father had come to school and fought the teacher.

---

*Glenn S. Pace, a retired cattle rancher, now lives in Mesa.*

# Depression Days

Ilo Waggoner

After attending Phoenix Junior College for one year, I transferred in 1925 to the University of California at Los Angeles. I concluded my junior year before I realized that the courses I was taking were not helpful in finding employment. During the summer I decided to become a teacher. During my senior year, I was able to enroll in a number of education courses, including student teaching.

My actual entrance into the teaching profession was the result of a number of unexpected happenstances. After working at a large California truck service station through the summer, I arrived back in the Valley on the first of September, 1929. After many inquiries, I learned that there were two positions open in Maricopa County. One was at Palo Verde District #49; the other in Washington School District #6.

I applied at Washington School, and Superintendent A. L. Jones offered me a contract at the close of the interview. I was to teach first, second, third, and fourth grade Mexican children, or whatever grade was assigned to me, drive a bus, and serve as scoutmaster. The salary was to be $1400. I felt very fortunate.

The scout troop did not have a very good scouting tradition. The teacher who had served as scoutmaster taught in the upper grades. After the graduation program in the spring, he had found his tires punctured, wires stripped from his engine, and water in his gas tank. "Uneasy and worried" is a mild description of my mental attitude when I was told about the situation by other teachers.

I had bought a new car, and picked it up after school on the day of the first scout meeting. As I approached the school I noticed the heads of several boys who were walking toward the school in the lateral that paralleled 27th Avenue. With great mental reservation I stopped and offered them a ride. They packed in—two deep. The conversation was lively and centered around the new car. When we arrived at school, I put the key in my pocket and started toward the meeting room. One of the older boys asked if I wasn't going to lock it.

"Why should I?" I asked.

"Someone might do something to it," was the reply.

I thought a moment and responded, "If someone wants to tear it up, they will do it even if it's locked."

The scout troop liked to go horseback riding across the desert north of Squaw Peak. They always provided me with a good horse, and I enjoyed the activity as much as the boys did.

Driving the bus was another matter. The bus body, as was typical for the time, had been built in Phoenix on a Dodge truck chassis. Hardwood seats had been built along the outside walls and the same kind of seats had been installed back-to-back in the center of the bus. It was noisy and uncomfortable.

The school nurse tried to keep me informed as to the children who should sit on the outside seats. This was to keep their heads from touching others as sometimes occurred when they sat on the center seats. The purpose of this little exercise was to prevent the spread of lice. It also taxed my diplomacy. Lice were not to be mentioned when a child was asked to sit in a certain place.

My class was an interesting challenge—all Mexican children—ages six to sixteen in grades one through four. I had a secondary certificate and had prepared to teach in high school. Segregation was not an issue. The arrangement of teaching Mexican children separately was common throughout the Southwest. It was a prac-

Families living under the Central Avenue Bridge in Phoenix. *Arizona Historical Foundation photo.*

tical way of dealing with a very real situation. The background of the Mexican people may help readers understand and appreciate this practice.

Mexican people resided in the Phoenix Valley at the time when the area was ceded by Mexico in 1848. They, however, were relatively few in number. They owned property and most of them spoke English fluently. The great increase in the Mexican population came during World War I, when laborers were brought across to do the work while United States men were in the army. Few of these immigrants could read or write in any language.

Field work and other manual labor provided them with an income. Cotton picking was the major work with the pickers being paid by the pound. Farmers liked to pay by check. Many of the Mexican people had to endorse the checks with an *X*. Merchants found they could take advantage of the situation, and they victimized the Mexican people. The farmers resented this, so they started paying with cash every time a picker weighed a sack of cotton.

The women and children could pick cotton and add to the family income. Since this was important to the Mexican people, it became a common practice throughout the county to allow those who wished to do so, to work until the Thanksgiving holiday. I was surprised the first year when over he Thanksgiving weekend the enrollment in my room increased from twenty to fifty-seven. For the most part, these children enjoyed school and were anxious to learn. With the help of other primary teachers, it was possible to plan activities and prepare work which kept them occupied. I imagine it was much like a one-room school. The older students helped, and I had the feeling that a good deal of learning occurred.

Schools often tried to work primary level Mexican children into the "regular" classes, but because of language problems and differences in the level of physical maturity it was not productive. However, children in the fifth grade and up were generally in integrated classes.

Teachers usually encouraged all children to continue

in school as long as possible, but at the same time they tried to create respect for the value of manual labor.

In the spring of 1932, Ed Ring, Principal of the Laveen School, announced his candidacy for county school superintendent of Maricopa County. He asked friends in the field of administration to recommend someone to serve as his assistant providing he was elected. I was suggested, and, of course, I enthusiastically accepted. The campaign was trying, interesting, and successful. January 1933 brought a new and challenging job.

The depression had been devastating to the schools and governmental services. Through the 1920s until now, the county office had maintained a textbook depository with a warehouse manager, provided a staff of attendance officers who divided their time among the various districts, and supervised the operation of the eleven "accommodation schools" in the outlying areas of the county. This total number of employees provided a patronage pool which was helpful during the primary election campaigns. However, Mr. Ring questioned the need for so many employees.

The state superintendent also maintained a textbook depository. Mr. Ring succeeded in getting the county depositories eliminated so that everything was handled by the state thus saving one salary and the warehouse rent. He also succeeded in getting the local districts to handle their own attendance problems through a bus driver or some other employee already on the payroll. The savings were significant. The county office— now manned only by the superintendent, his assistant, a secretary, a bookkeeper, and a warrant clerk— had to continue the management of the accommodation schools.

As a partial explanation for the continuation of accommodation schools, we need only look at the provision in the law which provided that county superintendents use money from the County School Reserve Fund to help defray the cost of transporting children attending accommodation schools and one- and two-room schools. In unorganized areas, many families existed on this small stipend—together with a little help from odd jobs. It was my responsibility to personally prepare the transportation vouchers for these people. The amount was based on an attendance report provided by the teacher of the school and the distance each child lived from school.

Warren Peterson, Chairman of the Board of Supervisors, owned the Flower Pot Ranch, located west of Arlington. He grazed cattle over much of the area served by the present Ruth Fisher School. While working on the transportation vouchers, I was often invited to attend a "Slow Elk Dinner" to be held in the area. Someone would have killed one of Mr. Peterson's cows. Mr. Peterson was aware of the situation, but as long as people used the entire carcass he didn't complain. Such an animal was worth only $25.00 or $30.00 at that time.

When the Works Progress Administration was developed, and able-bodied people were transferred from direct relief to the W.P.A. employment programs, the movement of people to the relatively inaccessible unorganized areas increased. They preferred direct relief. In justice to a few, I should also mention that there was some movement to areas where work relief was provided.

Depression conditions resulted in overwhelming problems for schools throughout the nation. In Arizona, we were perhaps a little better off than those states with large population centers and the severe unemployment brought to industry by the devastated economy. Wilson School district #7 was an example of the worst aspects of the Arizona situation. Because of Sky Harbor Airport, this district now has a very high assessed valuation per child, but during the depression years, it was approximately $815.00. The issuance of bonds was impossible. The school was maintained on the state and county apportionment which was $57.50 per child in average daily attendance for the highest six-month period.

The district's #7 indicates that it was one of the early districts established in the county. In the beginning it was a farming area, and as late as 1920, it was a pleasant middle-class community. After that, it deteriorated rapidly. Squatters moved in, built tar paper shacks for shelter, and, for the most part, joined the ranks of the unemployable.

In the late fall 1933, the truant officer assigned to that district came to the office to report a heartbreaking experience. The principal had asked him to check on children in one family because they were frequently absent. He finally found the shack where they lived. The mother had given birth to a little baby the night before. There was no bed. The dirt floor was covered with straw which provided warmth for the mother. The baby was wrapped in the father's shirt.

Mr. Ring called his friend, the sheriff, and within an hour we had a supply of food, bedding, and clothing gathered. Mr. Ring was starting out of the office door to deliver the material when a reporter from the *Phoenix Gazette* came in. He was greeted and, in spite of his protests, was ushered to the car to assist in the delivery. The secretary was directed to call the city editor to explain that the reporter had gone to Wilson School.

After the supplies had been delivered to the destitute family, they went on to Wilson School. The principal, G. S. Skiff, took them from room to room—each filled with 40 to 50 children; classes were also being held in the auditorium and on the stage.

On the way back to the court house, Mr. Ring explained why it would be impossible for that district to sell bonds to provide funds for the construction of additional rooms. He then confided in the reporter that he had been working with the county attorney in hopes of getting a legal opinion, that under certain circumstances, would allow school districts to use capital outlay funds in the regular budget to build classrooms.

I doubt if that reporter ever found out that the county attorney had called Mr. Ring to tell him that the reporter had picked the opinion off his desk and was going to write a severely critical—and perhaps justifiably so—article about the proposed misuse of funds. The article never appeared, and the reporter arranged to make a number of school visits to various parts of the county with Mr. Ring.

The depression made it impossible for many people, businesses as well as individuals, to pay their taxes. The warrants with which political subdivisions paid their bills had to be registered. These registered warrants earned 6% interest from the date of registration until the date they were called for payment. Teachers had to have money to pay rent, make car payments, etc. As a result they had to sell their warrants at a 25 percent or more discount. The legislature passed a bill requiring that pay-days should not be more than 16 days apart. This helped some because then teachers might get by without having to discount a full month's pay.

Mr. Ring offered to accept more than one voucher for each pay period. This would allow teachers to have warrants made in the exact amount of their rent or car payments etc. They could give these vouchers directly to their creditors thereby eliminating the practice of discounting salary warrants. This was of great help to the school people, but meant much extra work for the staff in the county school office. With the exception of Phoenix District #1 and the Phoenix Union High School District, each district issued an individual voucher for each warrant, and in most cases the school employee brought the voucher to the county office and waited while the warrant was prepared.

In order to overcome this situation, a cumulative voucher which could serve as a page in an auxilliary ledger was designed. After this was approved by the board of supervisors, the State Board of Education, and the State Examiner, it went into use in Maricopa County greatly reducing the clerical work. This voucher was later adopted by the other counties of the state. With revisions to meet legislative changes in budget requirements, this same voucher form has been computerized and continues in use today.

Another project illustrated the school activities of the time. This project developed visual aids programs. W. T. Machan, Superintendent of Creighton School District #14, was enthusiastic about the use of visual aids in the classroom. (The audio factor had not yet been developed.) Mr. Machan taught classes in the use of visual aids at Flagstaff during the summer school conducted there by the University of Arizona. Everett Johnson, Assistant Superintendent of Phoenix District #1, and Machan recruited a number of districts in Maricopa County to form a film circuit, rent films, and provide for their transfer from school to school. Martin Wist, a partner in the firm of Peterson, Brooke, Steiner, and Wist assisted in this venture.

Mr. Ring equipped his car with a special generator so that he could have the power to operate a film projector. He would drive his car as close as possible to school buildings where electricity was not available and show films. This gave the children in the accommodation schools an opportunity to see a large number of films that were helpful in the fields of history, geography, and health education.

Morale throughout the schools was extremely low. It reflected the pessimism of the parents. In the spring of 1934, the county superintendent decided to hold a county-wide elementary school exhibit. District exhibits had been quite common, but a county exhibit had never been undertaken.

The Valley Bank had moved from its old building on the north side of Adams Street between Central and First Avenue. This empty building provided a large, centrally located, exhibit room. Practically every school in the coun y responded. The building was filled with exhibits representing the full scope of the school activities. Public attendance was good—parents, teachers, and students developed a feeling of satisfaction. The worst of the depression was over, and a new enthusiasm spread through the schools.

---

*Ilo Waggoner retired in 1972 and lives in Tempe. The Waggoner School in Kyrene District is named in his honor.*

# Meeting the Minimum

Donald Magie Perkins

The country where I grew up was rough and rugged. It was 1940 before Arizona Highway 77 was paved between Showlow and Holbrook, and this was 20 miles from Clay Springs where we lived. My mother, Olive Magie Perkins, was a school teacher and having four children was one of her best qualifications because our attendance added at least ten percent to the state supported budget of whatever district she was teaching in. When she taught in the little red-brick, one-room schoolhouse in Shumway, there were only ten children, and without us the state wouldn't have allowed a separate school. I spent second and fourth grades (I skipped third grade) in this little school. One winter eight out of the ten students got whooping cough. The school board, faced with the prospect of having to close the school, decided that the eight children with whooping cough should come to school and the two who were well should stay home. Mom would stop and visit those two after school to check their assignments and give them instructions for their next day's work.

I started school in 1935 when I was five years old. We were living in Shumway, but Mom was teaching first grade in Taylor. For me to go to school with her solved the babysitting problem. My brothers were older and able to care for themselves. But after I had been in school for two or three months, my grandfather came to live with us, and Mom took me out of school.

I started again the following year. The school day ended at 2:00 p.m. for first graders, but the school bus did not pick us up until it came from Snowflake after high school was out at 4:00 p.m. This gave me more than two hours, so in nice weather I usually walked the five miles from Taylor to Shumway. Most days the bus would catch me before I arrived home.

One time I was just passing the Rhoton's place when their big yellow dog came charging after me. When the school bus came by a few minutes later, I was lying beside the road in an ant bed with red ants crawling all over me and blood soaked through my pants and shirt. My mother later told me she thought I had been hit by a car. My leg had been badly torn by the dog, and I was rushed to Doc Heywood in Snowflake. He pulled the wounds together with metal clamps. I don't know why he didn't use sutures. I still have the scars of those clamps alongside the scars of the dog bites.

Later when I broke my arm, the doctor, who did not have the benefit of X-rays, failed to diagnose the fracture. When a lump grew on my arm, I was brought to the doctor's office to have the arm rebroken and reset. My mother was to watch over the chloroform mask while my dad and the doctor rebroke my arm. The doctor absorbed in what he was doing, forgot the chloroform until Mom screamed that I had quit breathing. He frantically knocked off the mask and set about preparing a hypodermic syringe with which to give me a stimulant. Then with artificial respiration, he restored my breathing.

So there I was, back from the shadow of death with my arm broken again but still not properly set. It is crooked to this day.

---

*Donald Magie Perkins now lives in Vienna, Virginia and works as the Director of Finance for the Virginia Health Plan.*

# A Small Town Education

Morris Udall

When I enrolled at the University of Arizona in 1940 I felt sort of inferior because I was coming from the small town of St. Johns. There were only 80 of us in my graduating class, and I had to compete with students who had gone to the big schools in Tucson or to Phoenix Union High School, which at that time was the biggest high school west of the Mississippi. However, I soon learned that for someone wanting to be a lawyer and maybe a politician my early training had been fine.

My brother Stewart made a good point a few years ago in a magazine article where he said that school critics point out how today's children are "saturated with information but starved for experience." This was not a shortcoming in St. Johns because in addition to our formal schooling we all participated in the world of work. The instructors in this non-school school were our parents, older siblings, relatives, and assorted workmen. Projects were always underway in backyards and neighborhoods, and curious children were deliberately involved and given tasks to perform. In summers we went on roundups, joined in hay-baling, stripped beehives of honey, picked wild grapes for jelly, made molasses from sugar cane, and when a truckload of peaches would arrive in town we all helped bottle them. We were never quite sure where work ended and play began. For example, was it business or pleasure that made Stewart and Delbert Lee trap muskrats in a nearby swamp and sell the furs to a Chicago mail-order company?

I remember some excellent teachers from high school— Lawrence Sherwood in science and Letty Patterson in music. Mrs. Patterson was determined to get the whole town involved. My senior year she wanted a marching band. I don't remember the incident, but my mother often told how during the last football game of the season when St. Johns played Round Valley I had to run off the field (I was the quarterback), drop my helmet, and pick up my trumpet to join the band for half-time entertainment.

I thought nothing of it because this was typical of the way school activities were organized. I was not only on the football team and in the band, I was captain of the basketball team, had a part in the senior play, wrote a political column for the school newspaper, and on the weekends had my own dance band to earn spending money. Such participation wouldn't have been possible at a bigger school. Nevertheless, I didn't know enough to appreciate it.

At that time Arizona schools were not grouped according to size for athletic competitions. Our basketball team—a squad of eight or nine—won the right to represent our area in the state tournament by beating out schools from towns like Eagar and Lakeside. Then we came to Phoenix Union High School. Probably everyone on the team remembers the thrill of outscoring that big city school two-to-one. We hardly minded that we soon lost to another school and were out of the tournament. At the end when Duncan won our cheers were heartfelt. Duncan is a town even smaller than St. Johns.

---

*Morris Udall currently serves as a United States Congressman from Arizona, and in 1976 was a Presidential candidate.*

# Glimpses: 1920-1939

## THE HUMBLE BEGINNINGS OF THE DYSART SCHOOL DISTRICT
### Irene Marie Reed Ragsdale

I was nine years old in February of 1920 when my family moved from California to Arizona to raise cotton in the area where Dysart School is now located. My father cleared the land, and for two years we lived in tents. There was no school until Mr. Nat Dysart donated land. The school, appropriately named after its benefactor, was built in the summer of 1920. It was necessary to have eight pupils for a school, and since there were only six children living in the area a man with two children was hired to teach. Mr. Charles Mincks taught the eight of us—Charles and Mary Mincks, Mildred and Lawrence Dysart, Irene and Pearl Reed, and two others whose names I've forgotten. I was in the fifth grade and graduated in 1924. After attending high school in Peoria, I enrolled at Arizona State Teachers College where there were only about 500 students.

Cotton farmers were not very prosperous so I had to work to pay my college expenses. I worked forty hours a week in the library to pay for room and board. In addition, I did secretarial work for John R. Murdock, Professor of Social Studies. I was paid 25 cents an hour which was enough money to cover my other expenses. During that time Mr. Murdock wrote two books on Arizona government. I typed the manuscripts and did other typing and mineographing for his classes. When Matthews Library was completed I helped to move the library from Old Main.

After earning an AB degree in 1932, I applied for a teaching position at Dysart School. There were four teachers in the school which grew from such small beginnings twelve years earlier. My father, Dennie W. Reed, was on the Board of Trustees and had to resign to make it possible for me to be employed.

*Irene Reed went on to become a librarian. In 1938 she married Worthy W. Ragsdale, another Arizona educator. Now retired, they live at the Beatitudes in Phoenix.*

## THE THREE LITTLE SHEEPS
### Ann Nolan Clark

The first day I began teaching in a Bureau of Indian Affairs School on the Navajo reservation happened to be Columbus Day. At that time all B.I.A. schools had the same curriculum, and our lesson plans came prepackaged. I was supposed to tell the story of Columbus discovering America. I told the story the best I could and included details about the Nina, the Pinta, and the Santa Maria. Afterwards, according to the lesson plan, I was supposed to ask the children to draw pictures of the three ships. I did as I was told and was absolutely amazed when every child in the room drew three *sheeps* instead of three *ships*. We hadn't been communicating at all.

*Ann Nolan Clark, a well-known author of children's books set in the southwest, related this incident in a speech before the National Council of Teachers of English in 1972 when she was honored on her retirement after 50 years of working in BIA schools.*

## MY FIRST MAN TEACHER
### Richard Bridgewater

During the Great Depression men who were farmers and ranchers returned to the classroom as teachers. Teachers were not making much—$150 a month was usual—but, like it or not, that meant a lot to a near-bankrupt farmer.

Old Mr. Austin was not a man of finesse. The words "rough and ready" fit him well. He was our sixth grade teacher—our first man teacher. One day he kept the boys after class. He spoke in threatening tones, "Boys, I smell feet, and I don't like it. When you go home tonight tell your mothers that every boy must wash his feet and get on clean socks before class tomorrow. And I am going to check."

This news made my mother right angry. No son of hers ever had stinky feet. I insisted. I didn't want to risk Mr. Austin's eagle eye—or in this case, eagle nose.

The boys got the shoe-off test on Wednesday morning. That was our first lesson in the Austin tightship policy. It was quite a year. There were many boxed ears and kicks in the behind to help us grow up. "You understand now, don't you?"

The New Deal and things like price supports and FHA soon took those old guys back to their ranches.

*Richard Bridgewater grew up to become a teacher. He is now retired from the Phoenix Union High School System.*

## GETTING THE BASICS IN JOSEPH CITY
### Louise Tanner Gerber

My grandmother, Eliza Parkinson Tanner was one of the first school teachers at the old fort in the early days of Joseph City. However I did not give much thought to this when in the mid 1920's I attended elementary school in Joseph City with seven classmates. All eight of us graduated on May 12, 1927. Our diplomas were signed by the principal, the county superintendent, and three men on the Navajo County District Board of Trustees.

We were very proud of our beautiful brick school building which was completed in 1916 with four rooms and a library. A bond election for ten thousand dollars was passed by voters in November of 1914. The grounds boasted a swing set with four swings, a bar, one hand-swing, and two chains of equal length with hand grips. Also there was a slide and one giant-stride. At recess we played hop-scotch and/or marbles. We either brought our lunch in pails or walked home.

Bertha M. Rees was principal. She was very pretty with lots of charm as well as teaching capabilities. Although she was strict about homework and being attentive, she taught English with a flair. She lived in Holbrook where she was part owner of a cafe. The Joseph City townspeople liked her very much and often invited her to dinner. She did much to harmonize members of the Mormon church with non-Mormons. When Mrs. Rees came to our home she usually brought her husband and her daughter, Katharine. We were honored to have them as guests and always made special preparation so we could serve with more style than usual. Mrs. Rees inspired class members with the great American dream that we could do and become whatever we wished if we worked with determination. Our class motto was "No victory without labor." She also taught us to love America and be patriotic.

One year later when I enrolled in Owensmouth High School in California to begin the tenth grade, I scored very high in English, reading, and mathematics and was given all the necessary credits for the Los Angeles County High School System.

*Louise Tanner Gerber, whose family founded Tanner Construction Company, now lives in Tempe.*

## ON THE OTHER SIDE OF A SHEET

I started out at Madison School, but I had to leave it and go to the black school because they passed a state law. They had to provide separate facilities. Some districts we went with the whites, but then they said separate schools. Maybe a district would have just one black student, so they just hung up a sheet. Now if anyone from the State Department walked in, this little person knew to go behind the sheet. Then they were separated, so they provided their separate facility on the other side of the sheet as long as somebody was checking it. If no one was checking on them, then they just went with the rest.

*This statement was excerpted from "Lives of Arizona Women: Past and Present," an oral history project directed by Mary Rothschild, at ASU.*

## BEING A CRITIC TEACHER AT THE TRAINING SCHOOL
### Dorothy Robinson

In 1927 I applied to teach history at the Tempe Teacher's College. The position was filled, but Dr. Matthews said I could be a critic teacher in the fifth grade of the training school. I had not enjoyed my student teaching very much, but decided to give being a critic a try. I found as the year wore on that I really did like supervision. Being with children and having student teachers made me do my best, and something unexpected was always happening.

One time we wanted a really good nativity scene. This was in the old college auditorium. We got straw, bales of hay, and a manger. We painted props to give the desired setting. Then as a really nice touch we thought that live sheep would give authenticity to the scene. The college farm cooperated and brought in two or three of the animals. Only they weren't as docile as we had imagined they would be. Have you ever tried to make a sheep do what you wanted it to? We didn't repeat the idea the next year.

One winter we had a lovely fall of three inches of soft, fluffy snow. Everybody went crazy. The children had only slippers and socks on their feet so they were wet and cold. They would come in, warm up, and dry out before returning to the outdoor fun. Of course, while we were inside we managed to get a little work done, but the most important business of the day was playing in the snow. I don't remember that anyone became ill.

*The laboratory school on the ASU campus was closed in 1968 and many of its functions incorporated into area schools.*

Rural School woodworking class, 1921. *Tempe Historical Museum photo.*

## TEMPE RURAL SCHOOL AS SEEN BY A 1926 EIGHTH GRADER
### Kaseta Johnson

The Rural School is situated about three miles from town just off Southern Avenue. The school is connected with the Teachers College at Tempe and the senior students of the college are used as teachers in the school for practice. Rural which is the name of our school is surrounded with trees and has two base ball diamonds. The biggest part of the children at Rural are Spanish speaking. That is [because] the biggest amount of the population of the school district are the Spanish. Although there are about 21 white children. As for the teachers some know a good deal and some do not. Some are hard and some are easy. Altho we sure enjoy having them for teachers. For most of the year there were little social activity. All there was however was what the pupils themselves organized. We have had more parties the last part of this year than we had the first part. The national punishment of the Rural School is a bottle of caster oil, a ruler, and some soap, or sometimes we have to stay in at recess. The School also has a pet which is a cat. It is gray, has fleas and has sore eyes.

*Kaseta Johnson's handwritten essay is preserved in the Tempe Historical Museum where archivist Carol Moore copied it for this publication.*

## THE DESERT PAGEANT
### Velma P. Davis as told to Dana Shumway

I began attending Mesa High School as a freshman in 1936. I was shy and going to this big school scared me. My only consolation was having Harold, my brother, attend Mesa High at the same time. He was a senior and ever so popular so I didn't see him much, but it was reassuring to know that he was there.

In my graduating class there were approximately 350 students. Harvey L. Taylor was the superintendent. He was a very kind man and most of the students enjoyed knowing him. He had a strict rule that absolutely no one could walk, stand, or sit on the school grass. He wanted the grounds to be beautiful and they *always* were!

In the spring of 1936, Harvey Taylor directed his third outdoor pageant on the side of Superstition Mountain. A large majority of the student body participated, and I was lucky enough to be one of the dancers. We performed *The Leper* adapted from *The Home of Rummson* by Henry Van Dyke. I remember the hot, somewhat long drives out to Double Butte where we held our practices after school on the natural "stairs." I wore an Indian costume and I loved it. I never minded the practices, the heat, or the snakes. It was all so exciting. The only problem I had was attending practices and staying on top of earning my room and board. At times I would get behind with my work and the Skousens with whom I lived would get concerned, yet I always seemed to manage.

May 8, 1936, was the performance night. A generator was used for our lighting and a public address system was used for the main characters. A very large audience came to watch. Excitement was in the air, and those of us in the pageant were brought close together. When the last light faded into the desert darkness, another magnificent production had been added to the fame of Mesa High School, but the important thing for most of us was the friends we made.

*Velma Davis shared these memories with Mesa High School student Dana Shumway.*

## THIRTEEN YEARS IN THE SAFFORD SCHOOLS
### Helen Morris Bell

I was just looking at the picture of my eighth grade graduation from Safford Elementary School in 1937, and I realized that I still know more than half of the kids. They were my friends from kindergarten through high school. Friends and brothers and sisters all walked to school together—that is if the brothers would allow it. The only ones who rode buses lived a long way from school—out in what we called the cactus area. Also kids were bused into Safford from Solomonville. They were Mexican kids, and I don't remember that we felt prejudiced, although I know there was prejudice among our parents.

Practically the whole town were Democrats, but we had two Republicans in our class who loved to argue with one of the teachers. He would get so upset that his face would turn bright red. We really studied American Government because we had to pass the test on the National and the Arizona constitutions. The test was hard and there was no way to get around it.

Our home economics teacher once tried to answer a few of our questions about the facts of life. She was fired because some of the parents complained. They thought all sex education should be taught in the home. She wasn't even very frank; nevertheless she lost her job.

We didn't get to do nearly as much as the kids do now in the way of field trips, but did fun things like making maps out of papier-mache and going on picnics out in the clay knolls. When I was in the fifth grade I had my tonsils out. The class was studying how to write letters and the teacher helped each student write to me. I still have the letters which are hilarious.

There was lots of competition. We practiced penmanship in hopes of being selected to send a sample into a national contest. The top winners received an award. I didn't get one and I was crushed, especially since my best friend did, and I knew I wrote better than she did. We had spelling bees and music competitions. All the district schools would compete in glee club, band and orchestra, as well as solos. Ratings were given on each. Once our teacher took four students to Long Beach, California to compete.

Another thing we did was to compete fiercely for school office. My best friend and I competed for vice-president of the school, and she won by three votes. Later I was elected Ocotillo Queen, which was the homecoming queen, but I would rather have been vice-president. It meant more. Sometimes I think we got a better education than students do now. We got the basics and then built on them. There were opportunities for everyone to participate in something— assemblies, clubs, athletics, glee club, and orchestra or band. I worked in the office after school through the National Youth Authority program which gave part-time jobs to kids. I earned $6.00 a month.

*Helen Morris Bell now lives in Covina, California*

## RIDING BUS #3
### Lee Huber

I remember as a first grader in 1938 riding to school on old Bus Number Three. It came out of the mud holes along Southern Avenue east of Mesa and ground to a halt to pick me up on the canal bank. I had already walked a half-mile to catch the old yellow bird.

The body was constructed of wood. The seats were two long wooden benches on either side of the bus. The girls occupied one side and the boys the other. The windows were open slits along the sides with steel bars on them to keep the children from exiting through the sides. In cold weather, canvas flaps were lowered and buckled down over the open side areas. A long pipe ran down the center of the bus, and the exhaust fumes in the pipe served as our heater.

The old bus was very crowded. Not only did children sit on the four benches on each other's laps, but stood up in the center. When Bus #3 came to a stop there was always a pungent odor in the air. I've later identified it as dust, exhaust fumes, and burning brake fluid.

Bus #3 took us faithfully to and from school each day. I'm not quite sure how we survived, but those were the "good ol' days" and we loved it.

*Lee Huber now teaches eighth-grade science at Kyrene Junior High School.*

## MARTHA AND ROBERT KRAUSE: KING AND QUEEN OF THE DINING ROOM
### Ruby Harkey Schmieder

From 1913 to 1943, Robert and Martha Krause were the life blood of the Normal School dining room. Mr. Krause was the supervisor of all food and kitchen activities, and Mrs. Krause was the dining room matron.

Robert Krause was born in Hungary in 1877 and did considerable traveling and working in various hotels before coming to the Normal School. He was a slight, swarthy, and quick moving man with a Germanic accent. He showed a warmth toward students and co-workers that belied his efficiency. It is staggering to think that he was responsible for planning, buying for, preparing, and cleaning up after some 30,000 meals.

Martha Krause, a small prim, immaculate, red haired woman (some claimed the red hair was a wig) was a native of Scotland and traveled and worked with her husband before coming to the college. She ruled the dining room with a firm hand for she felt it was her duty to teach manners as well as to fill empty stom-

Third grade in Snowflake, 1929.

achs. Most students arrived with little or no knowledge of gracious eating. She found a simple way of enforcing her standards. She quietly dismissed the offender from the table. The unfinished meal and the disgrace of having to walk out guaranteed an immediate improvement.

I arrived at Tempe State Teachers College in the fall of 1927 with no funds but with the assurance of a job in the dining room to pay my board and room of $36.50 per month. Soon after I started to work, Mrs. Krause assigned me to serve the faculty table. I enjoyed this for it gave me the opportunity to know all the teachers and vice-versa.

The second year, I took Mrs. Krause's place as monitor of discipline and manners. Once I found it necessary to excuse a current boyfriend from the table. A custom that was hard to enforce was Mrs. Krause's method of eating a banana. It must be peeled, placed upon a plate, and eaten with a fork. The students claimed this was not a normal way to eat a banana.

The Krauses were extremely kind to me and often helped me by giving me overtime work, gifts, or clothes. As I bid them goodbye at the 1929 graduation, I said to Mrs. Krause, "I can never repay the kindness and help you have given me." She replied, "No, but you can pass it on to others." This remark has not faded in my mind even after these 55 years.

*Ruby Harkey taught in the Osborn School District from 1929-1937. In 1936 she married Carl Schmieder, a Phoenix jeweler. Their three children all attended Arizona schools.*

## MAMA AND THE P.T.A.

Magdalene Allen

Mama was an ardent worker in the P.T.A. She longed for cultural things and there were too few such events in our small town. Mama believed in making the P.T.A. interesting. At one special meeting, Mrs. Gammage, wife of the College president at Flagstaff, came to Woodruff and gave a reading of "Enoch Arden." Mother made chicken mousse for that meeting.

Mother was Woodruff president two years and later Navajo County president. It was through the P.T.A. that a culinary system was developed for the town of Woodruff, but mama died before she had running water in her own kitchen.

While she was County P.T.A. president, she hired someone to take her to Eagar, where she chartered the first P.T.A. in Apache County. Three of us had whooping cough. She was worried that the baby might choke, so she had me fix weak salt water. I was to give him a teaspoonful each time he coughed. I worried and worried, but everthing was all right—no complications, no trouble. He didn't cough once.

When she got home in the wee hours of the morning, she said her prayers had been answered. She was also happy that the people of Eagar had seen fit to form a P.T.A. The trip had been worthwhile. She had never been to Eagar before and was very impressed with the huge statue, "The Madonna of the Trail" that was standing in the middle of the intersection by the Federal Building in Springerville. Mother and her driver stopped on the way home, and as the lights from the car shone on it Mother got out and examined it. Her description left an indelible impression on my mind, and I was delighted to see it years later when going to a high school football game at Round Valley.

Mother was encouraged that the seed had been planted in Apache County, and so she began inquiring about also founding a P.T.A. in St. Johns. However the school principal from there called on Mama in Woodruff. She went out and sat in his black coupe where he told her he didn't go for P.T.A. and didn't want one there. Needless to say, Mother didn't especially care for him. This was unfortunate for St. Johns because, to my knowledge, no P.T.A. was organized there for nearly 20 years.

*Magdalene Allen, now a retired teacher living in St. Johns, wrote this as part of a family history. Her mother was Adeline Savage Pace who died from pneumonia in January of 1932.*

# 1940-1959: A Broadening of Horizons

This 1940 to '59 period was dominated by World War II and its aftereffects. Millions of Americans were forced into different lifestyles with different groups of people. Neither the United States as a country, nor these many individuals, could return to their old insulated ways of thinking.

Among the immediate effects of the war on Arizona schools, was that school boards had to find money for shovels, sandbags, and fire extinguishers. Children practiced safety drills by hiding under their desks. Patriotism was taught, and children brought their pennies and dimes to buy war stamps and bonds. In many cases, teacher were the volunteers who supervised the distribution of ration stamps for sugar, butter, shoes, and gasoline. Schools became collection centers for scrap metal and newspapers. The shortage of paper limited the publishing of textbooks, and in 1940-41, the State Department of Education collected and repaired 15,000 worn-out books to be recycled back into classrooms.

After the war, Arizona experienced tremendous growth. Soldiers, who had been stationed at desert airbases, came back with their families. As air conditioning improved, relatives and friends moved "out west" to join them, and so began the great exodus to the Sun Belt. In the late '50s, Phoenix and Tucson became the fastest growing cities in the United States.

What happened at Arizona State College in the winter of 1945-46 was a dramatic illustration of what the whole state would soon experience in varying degrees. Fall semester ended on a Friday in January with 553 students enrolled. When the spring semester began on the following Monday, 1,163 students appeared. By the next September, the figure had climbed to 2,180. Many of these students were returning soldiers going to school on the G.I. Bill of Rights. The elementary and high school increase was not quite so dramatic, but it was enough to tax—both literally and figuratively—the state's old time residents. State superintendent E. D. Ring noted in his 1946 report that Stanfield had only three teachers for its 212 students, Toltec had one teacher for 99 students, and Eleven Mile Corner had two teachers for 141 students. By 1952, over 5,000 children were attending double-session schools. Sixty percent of elementary classes contained more than 30 students while eight percent contained more than 40.

Out of necessity, efficiency and economy became more important than a feeling of community pride in the building of schools. The State Department of Education acted as a clearing-house of information on how other high-growth areas were solving school construction problems. Portable classrooms, prefabricated buildings, relocatable schools, and several schools built from the same or similar architectural plans were new concepts quickly adopted. Such creative problem-solving was necessary because the sudden influx of students came after a fifteen-year period of neglect to school buildings caused first by a lack of money during the depression and then by a lack of materials and labor during the war.

Another effect of the war was to push Arizona into what Marshall McLuhan would soon label "the global village." Arizona citizens came home from the war with expanded horizons. From now on, when something important happened in Washington or Russia, the reverberations would be felt throughout Arizona

THE WHITE HOUSE
WASHINGTON

May 21, 1942

My dear Mr. Studebaker:

Now that the school year is drawing to a close, I want to express to the school officials and teachers of the United States through you the appreciation of their government for the many special services rendered in the war effort. They have helped to bolster morale on the home front, have worked overtime in helping to register citizens for the Selective Service, as well as for sugar and gas rationing, and in many other ways they have assisted in civilian defense activities. I know that their cheerful and efficient service in these matters in addition to their main work in the schools and colleges, their uncomplaining overtime in the cause of freedom and democracy, have served to confirm the faith of the American people in the schools as a major bulwark of the Nation.

Very sincerely yours.

*Franklin D. Roosevelt*

Dr. John W. Studebaker,
United States Commissioner of Education,
Washington, D. C.

From *The Arizona Teacher-Parent*, October, 1942.

School patrons accustomed to classical Greek architecture complained about the "cattle-barn" look of the new Tempe Union High School built in 1953.

Patriotic First Grade Rhythm band, 1942.

Eighth grade graduating class, 1950. Kenilworth Elementary School in Phoenix.

schools. Contributing factors to this broadened view included new systems of mass communication, certification requirements for more and continuing education, a variety of professional organizations for teachers, and the increased mobility of teachers and administrators. In 1946, for example, 657 of the 920 teaching certificates granted by the Arizona Department of Education went to people moving in from out-of-state.

Obvious effects of the war on curriculum included an increased emphasis on teaching inter-American friendship and patriotism, health, safety, nutrition, conservation, and geography. During the early years of the war, over 8,000 Arizonans attended special classes held in the schools to train adults for civilian war-related work. Less direct effects on the choice of textbooks and decisions about how school time should be spent related to the anti-Communist ardor of the McCarthy era. A pro-science and technology enthusiasm developed in the late '50s when the National Office of Education published a two-year-study showing that Russian schools gave their children a more thorough training in science and math than did American schools. The launching of Sputnik added weight to this report, and in 1958 Congress passed the National Defense Education Act which provided money for schools to use in improving their offerings in science and math— later expanded to all basic areas of the curriculum. It was 1963 before most Arizona schools took advantage of this act because school boards feared that accepting federal aid would mean the end of local control.

Probably the most significant change to come out of this period was the official desegregation of schools as voted for by the state legislature in 1951. It's almost impossible to separate the philosophical from the practical reasons underlying this decision. State law had originally specified separate schools in any district where there were eight or more negro children. The figure was later changed to 25 or more. Before the late '40s, there was not a large black population in Arizona. The State Superintendent's report showed 457 black students in high school and 2,281 in elementary school. The 20 or so black elementary schools which were in the larger population centers of the state were mostly one-room schools with children being gathered from many miles around. Even though the facilities were generally of poor quality, maintaining these separate schools was a financial strain on districts which were struggling to meet expanding enrollments and keep up with post-war inflation.

A few districts tried to get more use out of their separate schools by also requiring Hispanic children to attend. In contrast, Indian children were welcomed, even recruited, into public schools where the Federal government would pay for their education. In 1940, 45 Arizona districts were receiving money for 583 Indian students; by 1947-48, 1,506 Indian children were in public schools, and by 1952 the figure had risen to 3,526. Part of the increase was caused by Indians moving from reservations into towns for available jobs, while another part resulted from tribes deciding to use the federal money to form their own schools rather than leave the management of their childrens' education to the Bureau of Indian Affairs.

In 1955 when the Supreme Court ordered that school desegregation should begin at once, many Arizonans thought the problem had already been solved in their schools. However, the ensuing years showed that the matter was more complex than simply closing down a few schools.

Miscellaneous accomplishments of this period include the 1943 establishment of a contributory state retirement plan for teachers, the 1950 passage of minimal safety regulations for school buses and the later establishment of qualifications for bus drivers, and the 1955 founding of the Arizona School Boards Association. In 1945 the legislature changed the University of Arizona Board of Regents to the Board of Regents of the Universities and State Colleges of Arizona. This helped pave the way for the two state colleges to become universities, Tempe in 1958 and Flagstaff in 1966. In the private sector, the American Graduate School of International Management began welcoming students in 1946 to the new campus it was creating out of the now defunct Thunderbird Airbase six miles north of Glendale. And in 1949 the Arizona Southern Baptist Convention welcomed students to Grand Canyon College in Prescott, later moved to Phoenix.

# From School to School

Claudia Ross

Ash Fork School where I started in 1936 was surrounded by a barbed wire fence to keep the cattle out. Stiles over the fences let the children—and the dogs—in. My teacher, being a patient person, allowed my dog to slip in and lie beside my desk. We had two classes in a room, and when we had more students than desks we sometimes sat two in a seat.

During recess, we were separated from the boys on the school ground . Boys played baseball. Girls played jacks and jumped rope. Later we also had baseball and volleyball teams.

Because of my father's work, we moved often. I learned how to make new friends and adjust to different schools. Arizona schools were considered more advanced than California's, and when we would move to California, I would be put into an accelerated group or moved a year ahead. When we returned to Arizona, I would be put back a year.

Girls did not wear slacks to school, so during the time I went to the eighth grade in Williams, I would put on a pair of boy's levis, tucking my skirt into them, and take turns "breaking trail" through the snow with a neighbor boy. At school I would slip out of the levis and roll them up until it was time to trudge home again. We lived about two miles from school, and walked every day.

We had lots of homework. Our parents wanted us to get good educations, so they were supportive of teachers and encouraged us to excel. They expected us to have school work to do at home, and the teachers never let them down.

While we lived on the ranch near Cornville in 1945 we were bused into school. There I met Miss Rayle. She taught Latin a good number of years, and had also traveled extensively. She opened our eyes to more than Latin helping us see the world as an interesting place. I can't remember much Latin today, but I can still remember some of the discussions we had in her class.

Winslow High School (1947-49) had a lot of spirit. The entire town supported the teams, and attendance was high at sports activities. The night before a game, the rally would feature a bonfire of railroad ties shaped into a "W" and wrapped with kerosene soaked cloth. Cheerleaders led us in yells, with each person trying to outdo the other. The rally ended with a chanting serpentine that wound through the streets of the town. Those who did not care to join the serpentine followed along behind combining their voices in the chants and songs. Alumni swelled the ranks of students, and we had the feeling that the whole town was supporting the team.

On "ditch-day" seniors had a special celebration. They were aided in their efforts by their class advisor and the school staff. The date was selected and carefully concealed from the underclassmen. We arrived at school early to load the buses and be on our way. Oak Creek was a favorite place to go.

Verla Oare stands out as my best teacher. She expected much from us. Most of us gave it. She trained us in doing research on a particular subject and then writing a paper on it. Her emphasis on thinking through an assignment, being thorough in research, and drawing conclusions carefully did much to prepare me for college and my future work.

She also helped to open my mind to the accomplishments of women outside the home. It seemed at the time that girls were being reared to be educated mothers. The boys were being reared to do something better than just work for the railroad as their fathers had done. All of us were being educated to fit into the corporate and political machines of our time. We didn't particularly know who we were. After all, no one had ever asked us, so we assumed there wasn't a question.

The harsh realities of the next three decades had not hit us. We thought we would marry and live happily ever after, rearing moderate families in a moderate community, with moderate incomes. Science fiction and pondering the future were diversions for the brainier ones, but far removed from our reality.

---

*Claudia Ross now lives in California. Her mother's story appears in the 1900-1919 chapter.*

---

## MILES SCHOOL AND MISS GIBSON

Renée Jácome Majors

It was in the early forties just before the disruption of things at the end of World War II when I walked to kindergarten at Miles Elementary School a half block from my home on the unpaved 12th Street. Classmates were to come from across the tracks, and across the arroyo, which seemed to divide Tucson's poor from the more affluent students attending Miles on the other side of Broadway. From those early days I seemed to be in the middle, comfortable in both societies, taking the best of both. One classmate had two sets of teeth. Dental health had not become a part of the curriculum. Another had never seen an indoor bathroom.

The Jácome families traditionally sent their children to parochial schools so the nuns arrived and sat in the living room asking my mother why I was going to public school. Politely they were dismissed, and as the only child of Art and Katie Jácome, I continued my "improper education" in the Tucson Public School System. I remained there from kindergarten through high school with the exception of a year in California during the war in which my father served. Miles School was a unique institution with more than its share of Tucson's complex society. There was no busing and no free lunch nor bilingual education. If we spoke Spanish in school we could be expelled.

No one who went to Miles could forget Miss Goldie Gibson, the fifth grade teacher. She had been my mother's teacher at Tucson High, and it became a family tradition to discuss Miss Gibson whenever conversation lagged. Her name would bring smiles which needed no words. Of special importance to her reputation was the green Model-T Ford which she shared with students on impromptu "field" trips. The car was as vital and priceless as its owner. To us, neither was ever old nor out-of-date.

Whenever we asked Miss Gibson when her birthday was she would reply, "Henry Wadsworth Longfellow's birthday." Our class looked up the date, and on February 27th after collecting our pennies we presented her with a small "gold" pin in the shape of her antique auto. From this experience, we learned how to accept a gift graciously. She thanked us, and delightedly placed the pin on the lapel of her gabardine suit where it remained the rest of the year. Stereotypically she looked the librarian with her erect posture, gabardine suit, and graying brown hair loosely pinned atop her head.

Miss Gibson never wanted to retire from teaching, and one day she came in to the Jácome's store and informed me that she had been forced to retire from the Tucson Public schools and was now proudly teaching at the Indian mission schools. Then, one evening, I met my former (not old) teacher at Frampton Stone Cafeteria, and she said she was selling her home, which had always been a favorite visiting place for her students, and was moving back to her birthplace in Huntington, West Virginia.

The last letter I received from her, written as usual in her beautiful unmatched penmanship, confided she was having a glorious time sledding with the children in the newly fallen snow of 1966. Some may have called her an "old maid school teacher," which was a phrase common in those days, but we children knew she was one Miss who seldom missed a thing.

*Renée Jácome Majors now lives in Montgomery, Alabama.*

---

# World War II in Show Low

Myrna Tanner Gibson

When Pearl Harbor was bombed in 1941, I was in the first grade in Show Low Elementary School, so it is not surprising that the war and experiences connected with it colored my early school years.

I still remember vividly, and with a certain chill, the feeling I had as my family listened to a broadcast on our old Philco radio and learned that the United States had declared war on Japan. Of course people all across America, including those in the little White Mountain town of Show Low, knew that entering World War II was the "right thing to do," and six-year-old Myrna Tanner knew it too.

Show Low, small in number of inhabitants, was large in patriotism. My family and most others grew Victory Gardens, bought War Bonds, saved tinfoil and scrap metal, and gladly accepted shortages and rationing as ways of helping America win the War. Mothers proudly and fearfully displayed banners with stars in their windows as their sons went to war, and some— too many— changed those stars to gold ones as their sons died in battle in places they had never heard of before the War.

Perhaps because of the War, the Pledge of Allegiance was more than words to me. I truly pledged my allegiance to the United States of America as I reverently spoke those words each day.

Air raid drills were a part of my early school years for we were taught to be prepared should we be attacked. The drills frightened me for Show Low was the center of my universe, and I didn't realize that it hardly qualified as a major bombing target.

Behind our four-room school, on the playground really, was a scrap metal depository. Mostly, it seems to me, there were old rusty cars which had been collected and were waiting to be sent elsewhere for re-use. We students found them fascinating. We organized ourselves into groups and each group laid claim to an old car which was then transformed into a comfortable "home" or "fort" or "office" with pirated tidbits from home. And, of course, we played "war." Playground activities were not very well supervised in those days.

Show Low Elementary School through most of the '40s was made up of four rooms with four teachers, each teaching two grades. I thought then we had the best teachers anywhere, and in retrospect I feel I was not far wrong. Phosia Smith, Ella Chlarson, Leora Kartchner, Ina Ellsworth, and Charles Whipple were exceptional teachers.

Although she never taught me, Ione Pearce Owens, who taught in Show Low for many years, was a model for me while I was a student at the University of Arizona. On discouraging days, I thought how her teaching certificate had helped her support her large family after her husband died. That made me feel a degree was the best possible insurance and made me keep going until I earned two of them.

Both my love for education and my patriotism have roots in Show Low Elementary School.

---

*Myrna Tanner Gibson is currently a student at ASU and plans to be awarded a degree in journalism in 1986, the same year her son graduates from law school.*

# Junior-Senior High School in the Gila River Relocation Center: 1942-45

Kinzo Yamamoto

This description of the Junior-Senior High School at the Gila River Relocation Center, Gila River, Arizona, is a collection of memories of my youth during my internment. I was eleven and one-half years old in March, 1942 and fourteen and one-half years old when released from Camp in April, 1945. During these years, as most students of World War II know, Japanese Americans were "relocated from the West coast States of Washington, Oregon and California (and a few from Hawaii)" under the aegis of Executive Order 9066 signed by President Franklin D. Roosevelt.

In order to describe the educational setting of the school, it is necessary to describe the place where we lived for over three years. The Gila River Relocation Center was comprised really of two "camps" of some 10,000 internees or prisoners of Japanese origin most of whom were American citizens. I lived in Camp 2 which was several miles away from Camp 1. The internees were housed in living units usually four families to a barrack. Fourteen barracks, plus men's and women's washrooms, a laundry room, an ironing room, a recreation room, and a mess hall made up a block. Over 100 blocks made up our camp.

These two camps were nestled inside the Pima Indian Reservation near Phoenix, Arizona. The Center was located in a desert environment which in all appearances remains the same even after the Center was closed.

The school in the relocation center was a collection of barracks arranged in rows with each barrack containing several classrooms. In each classroom there were wooden tables with attached benches similar to a picnic table. Some of them had linoleum tops on them. As with most barracks, the floor was made of wood and overhead you could see the rafters. A teacher's table and chair, a blackboard, and a "pot-bellied" stove comprised the rest of the equipment. Sashless and screenless glass windows provided most of the lighting because classrooms had only two bulbs.

The rooms were hot in the fall and spring and cold during the winter months. During dust storms we had to close the windows while silt colored the air in sepia tones. In the winter, as the mood often struck us, somebody would pop a piece of gum eraser in the pot-bellied stove. The ensuing stink would nearly always drive us out of the classroom.

Teachers were a mix of Japanese American or "indigenous" residents who presumably were credentialed prior to internment and others, i.e., whites or non-prisoners. I do not know where these "others" came from, but in retrospect as an adult, I suppose the War Relocation Authority, the Federal agency which ran the Centers, must have advertised in some way. They, as a whole, were generally older, maybe retired school teachers who were willing and able to teach those of us who were interned. Might I say that the instruction we received was better than that which I received throughout the rest of my high school, undergraduate, and graduate education. These teachers who came from the outside into the relocation centers must have brought with them a quality of human compassion coupled with subject matter competence that I am sure we school children did not fully appreciate. If any of them should read this document, may I say thank you Mr. Sturgis (mathematics), Mrs. Edwards (English), and Mrs. Sawyer (human biology) — to list a few whose names I still recall after 42 years.

In the Junior-Senior High School, each student was

A high school class at the Gila River Relocation Center. *Arizona Historical Foundation photo.*

assigned a faculty advisor who had to review and authorize the set of classes that each student chose. Classes were available much as on most modern college campuses in which a student could choose the teacher and time for courses. To register for a class, a student had to obtain the signature of the teacher who then officially placed the student's name on the roster of that class. It was not uncommon for an eighth grader to be taking algebra with freshmen and even seniors. A clanging bell sounded the end of a 50-minute class, and we had 10 minutes to go to our next class.

As I recall, although there was physical education, most of the team sports such as football, baseball, or basketball were organized either around residential blocks or by prelocation community-of-residence. These activities were independent of the school.

There were shop classes for the boys and home economics for the girls. Everyone at the junior high level took art and music.

There were school dances and proms including the crowning of kings and queens at some of these special occasions.

There were commencements. I remember going on the stage to get my diploma after having completed the eighth grade. For that occasion I was given a new shirt and I borrowed my brother's jacket. Male senior graduates who were 18 years or older and able-bodied were drafted. Also many enlisted.

This brief recollection of the school system in one relocation center as remembered through the eyes of a 14-year-old most assuredly can be enriched by older student-internees. The academic subject matter was richly taught, but the amenities of the schools we left behind were but memories. There were no swimming pools, acoustically sound theaters, or well equipped industrial shops. But, we took what was there and that experience will forever be part of the personal history of myself and of those with whom I was interned.

---

*Kinzo Yamamoto now lives in Fairfax, Virginia and works in Washington, D.C. for the federal government.*

# A School Board's Courageous Decision

Mary Ishikawa Tanita

I grew up feeling that my family, the Ishikawas, were well known and respected in Mesa. This was partly because of my older brother, Zedo Ishikawa, who was a star athlete for Mesa Union High School. He died when he was seventeen-years-old as a result of a shooting accident. His dying words were a message to the football coach and the team to play the opening game without him—to "carry on." The words became the school slogan, and every year my family presents a trophy in Zedo's memory to an outstanding Mesa athlete.

In 1941, I was a senior at Mesa High, and the day after Pearl Harbor was bombed I was frightened to go to school. I didn't know what would happen or how people would feel. However, I did go, and our American History teacher, Holland Melvin, without looking at anyone in particular or mentioning any names, told the class that the people of Japanese ancestry who were born and living in the United States had nothing to do with the bombing of Pearl Harbor and should therefore not be made to suffer from prejudice. I have never forgotten that moment of support at a time when I felt so unsure.

A few months later in the spring of 1942, the FBI told Mesa High that no students of Japanese ancestry could attend the school. An imaginary line dissected the valley, and Japanese people were not allowed to cross the line. Mesa Union was on the other side of the line so I could not go to school. In a way I was glad because I was still somewhat frightened, but I was sorry to miss graduation. The principal brought my diploma to me at home. I went to the baccalaureate services because they were held in a building north of the invisible line.

My future husband was a student at North Phoenix High School, and he had to find another school to attend. Members of the Japanese community in the valley represented by Bill Kajikawa of Tempe (who recently retired from many years of coaching at ASU) went before the Peoria Unified School Board to ask that Japanese students be allowed to attend school in Peoria. They agreed to this request and that is where my husband and most of the other Japanese kids finished high school. Although the matter was handled with little fanfare, it was extremely important to the lives of many young Japanese. We were grateful that we did not have to relocate to one of the camps, but talking about it is difficult. Old wounds heal slowly.

Forty years later, the local Japanese community remembered this incident and decided to honor the school board's courageous decision. The Arizona Chapter of JACL (Japanese American Citizens League) presented $5,000 as a gift to the Peoria School District. The administration was surprised because they had not been aware of the earlier incident. When they checked the 1942 school board minutes they found only two sentences:

> The American-Japanese high school students from the restricted military districts through Kajikawa of Tempe were asking permission to attend high school. On motion by Mr. Coor, seconded by Mr. McFrederick the Board voted to admit the students on trial.

---

*In 1912, the Ishikawa family came to Lehi to farm. Mary Ishikawa Tanita now lives in Glendale.*

# Being Black in the 1940s

Coy Payne

I came to Arizona in January of 1942. We landed in a cotton camp in Eloy where we remained until April or May—just long enough to earn money to buy a 1929 Model A for transportation. After we bought the car, we moved to a ranch five miles south of Chandler so that we might be close to a community with a good school system. My mother and my father, who was a former school board member, were determined that my brothers and sisters and I should have at least a high school education. Little did we know that we would be denied the opportunity to attend school in Chandler and would be bused to an all-black elementary school in Mesa, thirteen miles from where we lived. Mesa's high school was integrated, but only for students living in the city.

We rode the bus from Chandler Heights to Mesa, and back, for the balance of that year. The next year Mesa either refused to take Chandler children, or Chandler decided to accept the responsibility of educating black children who lived within its school district. In the little cotton farming community of Goodyear about five miles south of Chandler, the Chandler School District contracted with a land company to use some of its office buildings as classrooms; thus was born the first Chandler school for blacks. Walk-in students came from the nearby cotton camps and ranches. Those living too far away were out of luck and could not attend. Those living in Chandler proper were bused in an interesting venture which far surpassed most busing problems of today. Black children were brought from Chandler to Goodyear each morning, and Anglo and Hispanic children from the Goodyear area were bused on the return trip to schools in Chandler. In the afternoon the procedure was reversed. At Goodyear, the teachers were black, but the principal, superintendent, and board members were Anglo.

There were no school plans for blacks beyond the eighth grade. Black parents had requested that their children be allowed to attend Chandler High School, but the request was denied. One school board member became very adamant stating that he would "never allow blacks to sit in the same classroom" with his children. Later, the Chandler district negotiated with Phoenix Union High School district for black students to attend Carver High School in Phoenix. The Chandler district had to pay tuition and also provide transportation. The Sun Valley Bus line, part of the public transportation system, was used for a fifty-six mile round trip per day. The cost must have been substantial. The time involved was astronomical, and many students missed out on an education because they did not feel they should make such a sacrifice. One could not participate in athletics or other extra curricular activities when the objective had to be catching a bus to get home. Yet, that was a time for dedication and determination from students and parents. Graduation from high school was a goal that was uppermost in our minds—and graduate we did!

---

*After Coy Payne graduated from Carver High School, he went on to Arizona State University. He is now Assistant Principal of Chandler Junior High School.*

# Honor Roll: 1940-1959

**Willard Abraham**

A prolific writer and an enthusiastic teacher, Abraham came to ASU in 1953 where he was chair of the special Education Department for 23 years.

**John Armer**

Armer served on the Madison School Board from 1949-58 and on the Phoenix Union High School Board from 1961-68. He helped establish the Arizona School Boards Association and encouraged the use of citizen advisory councils. He participated in the Eisenhower White House Conference on Education and in the National Citizens Council for Better Schools.

**Robert Ashe**

Former superintendent of Peoria, Yuma, and Glendale public schools, Ashe joined the ASU faculty in educational administration in 1955. He was nominated for being an "exemplar mentor and distinguished teacher for multitudes of practitioners."

**Bertha Holmes Autenrieth**

Autenrieth was nominated first for what she has contributed to music education in Arizona and second for her part in successfully challenging in the early 1940s the legality of school board rulings against married women being teachers.

**Raymond E. Booth**

Booth taught in the Winslow schools from 1929-71, serving as superintendent beginning in 1939. Appointed to the State Board of Education by Governors Pyle and Fannin, he was recognized as a leading authority on school law.

**Trevor G. Browne**

A member of the Phoenix Union High School Board for 30 years, Dr. Browne exhibited a life-long commitment to public service.

**J. R. Cullison**

As director of the Arizona Department of Vocational Education, Cullison was the leader who fostered vocational education in the transition years following World War II.

**Roy P. Doyle**

From the position of principal in the Madison District, Doyle was recruited to be principal of the Payne Laboratory School. He was nominated for being "always humane, always effective, and always innately modest and wise."

**Walter Douglas, Jr.**

Douglas has been a member of the Flowing Wells School Board since 1942 and president since 1950—the longest tenure of a school board president in the United States.

**Curtis D. Greenfield**

Principal of Julian School from 1950-74 and Assistant Superintendent of Roosevelt District from 1974-76, Greenfield was nominated for being a tireless champion of disadvantaged children. After his retirement, he continues to substitute teach on a daily basis.

**Edith Haner**

Haner taught in Arizona high schools for 44 years. From 1937 until 1977, she was chair of Business Education at Phoenix Union High School.

**Taylor T. Hicks**

A member of the Prescott School Board for more than two decades, Hicks helped form the Arizona School Boards Association in 1949. He was Vice President in 1955 and President in 1956 of the National School Boards Association.

**William M. Kajikawa**

Bill Kajikawa joined the Arizona State Teachers' College physical education faculty in 1937 and continued coaching there for nearly 50 years. A leader in the Japanese-American community, in 1941 he helped arrange schooling for American-born Japanese.

**John Koerner**

An outstanding high school teacher of social studies in Glendale (1945-49) and in Phoenix (1950-82), Koerner modeled what he taught by working within the Arizona and the National Education Associations to promote desegregation and the open and free discussions of controversial issues.

**Letife Koury**

Koury taught in Holbrook from 1928-73 and served on the school board from 1976 to the present. She was nominated for giving "uncountable hours of her time tutoring underprivileged students" and for promoting better facilities and improved university preparation for students.

**Thomas Lee**

Former superintendent of Tucson Unified School District, Thomas Lee helped to identify and write desegregation guidelines.

**Henry Leim**

Superintendent of the Clifton Schools from 1927-45, Leim came to Phoenix to be superintendent in the Washington District from 1945-55. He provided the training and leadership which transformed a basically agricultural area into Arizona's largest elementary district.

**David D. Lloyd**

An administrator from 1953-84 in the Mesa School District, Lloyd helped write and promote state legislation to ensure schooling for handicapped students.

**Guy D. McGrath**

Founding Dean of the College of Education at ASU, McGrath served from 1950-68, during which the college grew into one of the largest in the nation. The I.D. Payne Laboratory, the Center for Indian Education, and the Reading Center were founded; Farmer Education Building was constructed, and the first Ed.D. and Ph.D. degrees were awarded.

**Robert Morrow**

As superintendent of Tucson Unified School District, Robert Morrow gained national recognition by successfully integrating Tucson schools in 1951-52, three years before the Supreme Court decision made segregation illegal.

**Scott "Chief" Nelson**

A journalism teacher at Phoenix Union High School, Nelson is credited with having launched several careers including those of Steve Allen and Bill Mauldin.

**Harold D. Richardson**

Richardson helped found the ASU College of Education Counseling Department. He served as the University's Academic Vice President and after the death of Grady Gammage was acting president of the University.

**W. A. Robinson**

One of the first things Robinson did when he became principal of Carver High School in 1945 was to recruit teachers with master's degrees and to upgrade the facilities and equipment at the school. When Carver students were integrated into the Phoenix Union system in 1955, Robinson became assistant superintendent.

**Fra Weinacker**

Director of Instruction and Assistant Superintendent in Phoenix Elementary District #1 from 1930-70, Weinaker led the district to be the first in Arizona to hire a full time psychologist and to establish special classes for children with special needs.

# Teaching Art at Carver High School

J. Eugene Grigsby, Jr.

In college, I resisted taking education classes. My father was a high school principal and my mother a primary teacher. I was determined to do something different, but we don't always know what the future will bring.

I majored in art at Morehouse, a College of Atlanta University, and then went on to earn a degree at Ohio University and to be an artist-in-residence and instructor at a couple of colleges. When the war came, I volunteered for service. Afterwards, I needed a job. W.A. Robinson, who had been a classmate of my mother and who remembered me from when he was principal of the Atlanta University Laboratory School, had come to Phoenix in 1945 to be principal of Carver High School. He wrote and offered me a job teaching art.

I didn't know where Phoenix was and had no interest whatsoever in going that far away from my family in North Carolina. But Robinson kept calling; in fact he sent a contract which offered me double my old art instructor salary. My family by then included a wife, a young child, and a baby. We were living with my parents and that house was getting crowded! So in 1946 I came to Arizona for $2,800 a year.

No art had been taught at Carver, and students had to be recruited. I really worked at it because Mr. Robinson told me if there were not enough students to "make" the classes, I would have to teach math or English. One student was signed to take art with the promise that he could drop the class if he really didn't like it. After the first week, he said he didn't like it, he wanted out. I said, "The agreement was you would try something, you haven't done anything yet!" So he stayed another week. The first day he tried a drawing. Threw it on my desk because he didn't like it. The next day he did a watercolor, and didn't like that either. The next day the same thing happened. And then on Friday he watched me pour plaster into a milk container and wanted to know what I was going to do with it once it hardened. I told him we were going to carve it. He was intrigued—probably because he had been carving on desks since kindergarten. He took one of the cartons home and on Monday brought back a carved figure. He never asked to get out of art class again! Later, when he was absent from other classes, they knew where to find him—in the art room! He dropped out of school his senior year and went in the army. He got into food service and traveled all over the world with one particular general. Practically all he did was ice carving. He is retired now, but whenever he needs some money he can make a cool thousand by doing an ice carving for a big banquet or reception.

My first year at Carver, Rip (Roosevelt) Woods was a freshman. He was one of those who would do more in three days than most of the other students could do in three weeks. When idle, Rip created problems, so to keep him occupied I put him to work on a mural depicting the life of the school's namesake, George Washington Carver. In researching for that mural, Rip discovered that Carver had wanted to be an artist, but Iowa State had denied him the opportunity to take painting classes and directed him into agriculture instead. Carver was in his senior year before being allowed to enroll in a watercolor class. Four of his paintings were selected for the 1893 World's Columbian Exposition in Chicago where one received honorable mention.

Rip's brother, James Woods, was interested in photography and later became a teacher at Brooks, a prestigious professional photography school. Another Carver student, Melvin Gray, was very interested in silk screening and is now in charge of all the advertising graphics for the Bayless stores. The best thing about teaching at Carver was seeing the kids grow and develop. Of course that happens in any school, but because so many of the Carver students came from the inner city and from very poor families, their growth was especially dramatic. Many of them had opportunities that they would not have had in other schools where they would have been in the minority and might not have been as encouraged to try out for plays or work on various projects, etc. Carver was small with only 400 students—all black. The teachers were black too except for the Spanish teacher. Robinson felt Spanish should be taught by a native speaker.

A biology teacher and I developed different kinds of projects together. Students would make drawings and paintings of biological systems such as the vascular system or nervous system. One girl made a set of teeth, another made an eyeball out of clay. A boy who had an assignment for an English class to write a 200-word theme about a character in a play couldn't seem to write that theme. So the teacher let him paint a portrait of the character. The picture won a National Scholastic award. He then turned around and wrote a 400-word theme about the picture he painted. These interrelated assignments, adapted to the special needs of individual students, were possible partly because Carver was a small school and also because of W.A. Robinson and his philosophy of education. He insisted that parents and students be included in faculty meetings and decision-making.

In 1954, a year before the Supreme court's desegregation ruling, Carver was closed. People felt that even though there were many opportunities at Carver, an integrated school would be better for black students. Certainly no one could argue about us having a bad location. It was right behind the railroad tracks. The noise of the trains as well as the airplanes from nearby Sky Harbor would continuously drown out whatever a teacher was saying. And the school board thought the cost per student was too high because we were the smallest school in the district and yet had the best equipment and the best prepared teachers.

When Carver was closed, most of the students went to Phoenix Union, others to Phoenix Tech. Mr. Robinson insisted that the teachers be scattered throughout the school district so that Phoenix Union did not become just another Carver. In 1946 when I arrived in Phoenix, Carver teams were not allowed to compete with other schools. When Carver closed eight years later, our teams not only competed but were state champions in all major sports. The first year Phoenix Union had practically an all-Carver football team.

Phoenix Union High School District Art Department faculty meeting.

Art teachers from the other schools wanted most of the equipment from the Carver Art Department. Some of it went with me to Phoenix Union. However the administration decided the Exacta camera was too expensive and sophisticated for high school students. It was sent to the Phoenix College art department. A year or so later I borrowed that camera. The housing was loose, the edge of the lens was bent—it was a mess. We had been using it at Carver with no problems for at least five years.

---

*J. Eugene Grigsby, Jr. completed his Ph.D. at NYU in 1963 and in 1966 joined the ASU School of Art.*

# Phoenix Union High School: Crossroads of the Fifties

Alleen Pace Nilsen

Because my family lived on the "wrong" side of McDowell, when I graduated from Kenilworth Elementary School in 1950 I had to go to Phoenix Union High School. Most of my classmates went to the new and therefore more exciting West High while a few went to North, which being near the Phoenix Country Club had its own kind of elegance. However, I soon adjusted to my fate of going to "old P.U." and learned to appreciate the fact that partly because of its downtown location and partly because of its heritage, it was at the center of things.

Students were required to take one non-solid subject: phys. ed., band, chorus, or miscellaneous classes such as teacher's aide. I was too shy to get undressed in front of other people so I wouldn't take P.E., and I was too unmusical to sing or play an instrument and so I couldn't take a music class. This left being a teacher's aide. I ended up working in the Dean of Students' office where I was often involved in the events of the day.

In 1953 just before my senior year, the Phoenix Union High School Board took a step toward integration by giving black students who were attending George Washington Carver High School the option of attending one of the district schools. Because of where they lived, most of the black students who transferred from Carver came to Phoenix Union. Integration was rapidly becoming a national issue, and Phoenix Union received lots of publicity. Arizona free-lance writer Joseph Stocker sold a story to LOOK Magazine, and a crew arrived to do a photographic essay. I was one of the students escorting the photographers around the campus and getting my picture taken. I always felt a little guilty about the matter—I think a lot of us did—because we didn't associate with the black kids except during that one week There were no blacks in any of my classes and so there wasn't an easy or natural way to get to know them. Perhaps most of the seniors stayed at Carver to graduate with the main body of their classmates. At least the few dealings I had with black students were positive.

I can't say the same for what in the previous year had been a less successful social experiment. In 1953, Governor Howard Pyle directed the state's highway patrolmen in a nightime raid on the small, isolated community of Short Creek located on the Arizona-Utah border. An off-shoot group of excommunicated Mormons had been living and practicing polygamy there ever since it was outlawed in 1895. The way the raid was handled was extremely controversial and contributed to Governor Pyle's defeat the following November. At the time, it made headlines in both local and national newspapers. Arizona has many old Mormon families, including mine, whose ancestors practiced polygamy. Most of us felt varying degrees of embarrassment—sort of a shared responsibility—over these people and their life style.

Shortly after the big event while I was in my first hour class, a note came to the teacher asking that I be sent to the Dean's office. When I got there, I was introduced to two girls from Short Creek and asked to escort them around the campus for their first day of school. Apparently they had been taken into state custody and placed in foster care. With my help, they were now expected to become typical teenagers.

I was mortified by the thought that I had been chosen as their escort because the administration knew I was Mormon and therefore thought I had something

Scott Nelson and a PUHS journalism class on a field trip to *The Arizona Republic* and *Phoenix Gazette* print shop, 1953.

in common with them. Both girls wore long dresses, not the glamorous kind seen in western movies, but limp and faded cotton prints. Their hair was braided, one girl's wrapped around her head. Their skin was ruddy from the sun and had obviously never seen make-up or hand lotion. Their shoes and socks were "country."

The thing I remember most was how terrified they were. I tried making conversation, but they kept their heads down and would only nod or mumble, and they wouldn't establish eye contact. I felt sorry for them, but at the same time my teenage instincts for social survival made me want to demonstrate that these two were as alien to me as they were to everyone else. It was a miserable day. I've no idea what happened to the girls, but they were at Phoenix Union only that one day. Someone must have realized the hopelessness of the situation and figured out a better plan.

If a similar incident happened today, I doubt that it would be nearly as traumatic. In the 1980s, most people are fascinated with the unique or unusual, but in those pre-television days we were cloistered and very suspicious of anyone who dressed or acted differently from us. One year when January rolled around, a new teacher who had come from someplace like Indiana or Iowa began wearing gloves and an overcoat. We thought the sight so funny that after school we would watch for him, point him out to other students, and snicker. Umbrellas were another thing we thought hilarious. Only a dude would be such a pansy as to use an umbrella.

One day Miss Lois Arnold, who taught junior-year English, must have gotten fed up with our smug parochialism because out of the blue she asked if any of us had been east. I proudly volunteered that I had been to Chicago. She hooted that Chicago was the gateway to the west. To drive the point home, she quoted some line from Carl Sandburg. I fumed the rest of the period wavering between humiliation and indignation. I wanted to argue that with two-way traffic her gateway to the west could also be my gateway to the east.

We were fascinated with the personal lives of our teachers, and we joked about the friendship between the social studies teacher, Doc Ogle, and the English teacher, Mila Bray. It was an exciting day when someone came to school and reported that she had found an autograph in her mother's yearbook that was signed "Yours till Doc Ogle marries Miss Bray." There was something reassuring about this cross-generational bit of communication. It made us feel like our little part of the world was safe from change. We vowed to begin signing our yearbooks that way too, but by the following May we had forgotten. Several years later when I was married and living in what even Miss Arnold would have agreed was "the east," I got a letter from home that brought the memory back. Doc Ogle was in the hospital dying from cancer, and Miss Bray had come to the hospital where a wedding ceremony had been performed. I later saw her name printed as Mila Ogle, so the marriage must have really taken place.

Our window to the world was the journalism classes taught by Scott Nelson. We called him *Chief* as in *Editor-in-Chief*. Out of the junior year journalism classes, he would pick seven or eight students to form the nucleus for the staffs of the *Phoenician* yearbook and the *Coyote Journal* newspaper. I was in this group in 1953-54. One of us would be campus reporter for the *Arizona Republic* and another one for the *Phoenix Gazette* while someone else was the photographer. The downtown papers paid us $5.00 for each photo they used and 20 cents a column-inch for stories. There weren't so many high schools in the valley and so the papers welcomed both news and features. The offices were only a few blocks from school and we would drop off stories two or three times a week. Earnings ranged between $35.00 and $50.00 a month depending on whether we got away with double charging through measuring the photos in with the column-inches of writing. Chief Nelson wouldn't have approved of this bit of deviousness, but he didn't interfere with our private dealings with "the real world." He opened doors for us and dropped suggestions, but we never felt pressured or supervised by him. In the spring of 1954, Dean Martin and Zsa Zsa Gabor were in town making a movie at the State Fairgrounds. I went out and interviewed them. Looking back, I imagine it was probably Nelson's idea, but at the time it never occurred to any of us that he should get credit for the exciting things we students were doing.

In 1976, the Phoenix Union High School District published a commemorative history. As a foreword, the editor solicited letters from the district's two most distinguished alumni, cartoonist Bill Mauldin and performer Steve Allen. They both mentioned Scott Nelson. In 1941, Steve Allen was assistant editor of the *Phoenician* and credited Nelson with getting him a scholarship to Drake university where he studied radio production. When Bill Mauldin attended Phoenix Union from 1937 to '39, he concentrated so much on his art classes and on drawing cartoons for the *Coyote Journal* that he failed his other classes and wasn't allowed to graduate.

In 1954 he came back to see Chief Nelson. We knew he was coming and could tell from Nelson's excitement that he was someone the world respected. Although we had been too young to appreciate the famous "Willie and Joe" cartoons, we did know what a Pulitzer prize was. Nelson told us how Mauldin hadn't been allowed to graduate but how in 1945 Nelson had wrangled a post-dated diploma so the school could claim its own.

When Mauldin arrived at the journalism room, Chief Nelson pulled out his old drawing board for an autograph. I don't think the board had been intentionally saved; schools just don't replace such things very often. Those of us included in this visit appreciated the opportunity of meeting a student who had succeeded, but actually we were disappointed. We knew that he had come directly from the airport, and we were amazed that he was dressed so casually. I can't remember if he was actually wearing old army clothes, but I do remember they looked like army clothes, and he carried a duffel bag for luggage. Today that's in style, but in the early '50s we couldn't believe that anyone famous wouldn't also be rich or that somone rich wouldn't want to look rich.

Another visitor who most of us didn't know enough to appreciate but who we could tell from Chief Nelson's respect was someone we should admire was Margaret Bourke-White. A couple of months after the photographers from *LOOK Magazine* had done their piece she also came to take pictures of the newly integrated school. I escorted her around the campus and was amazed at the contrast in working styles. She was so careful in setting up each picture that she probably didn't use more than two rolls of film in the two days she was there. The *LOOK Magazine* team had shot pictures in every possible direction. They must have had 400 prints to choose from. I was so impressed with the difference that I still categorize people's working methods as either "the Margaret Bourke-White" or "the *LOOK Magazine*" approach.

There were over 4,000 students at PUHS, but the same group of fifty or sixty kids were always in my classes. I'm sure we were tracked or grouped, although in the days before sunshine laws required schools to release such information, it was never discussed. Nevertheless, by the time we were seniors we began to wonder, and one of us who worked in the registrar's office discovered little numbers written in red ink on our cards: 132, 121, 114, 118, etc. We engaged in a fierce debate as to whether these might be our I.Q. scores. Those with the higher numbers said yes; those with the lower numbers said no. Graduation interrupted our argument, and we went our various ways never knowing for sure whether or not we were bright. To get the answer, we had to venture forth and test ourselves against the world—probably as good a method as any.

# Becoming an Artist

Lois D. McCarty Banks

I was a high school sophomore in 1951 when my family moved to Phoenix from southern California. There were two months left in the school year, and my dad hoped I could make friends at school and avoid a lonely summer.

Bethany Home Road was the northern boundary for Phoenix high schools, and our new home in the northernmost housing development in the valley was one block over, so I had to enroll at Glendale Union High School, seven miles away. I caught the school bus on the corner of Nineteenth Avenue and Bethany Home Road near a stable where Phoenix Baptist Hospital now stands. A farm house occupied the southwest corner (now 300 Bowl), and ChrisTown Shopping Center was a large cow pasture lined with tamarisk trees.

The ride seemed short over the narrow two-laned roads as we passed Japanese-grown fields of giant strawberries, open irrigation ditches, huge cottonwood trees, and more farm fields. The highlight of the trip was the aging, brick sugar-beet factory that loomed up at Fifty-first Avenue and Glendale. I braced for it each day imagining it to be a nineteenth century insane asylum.

Three things impressed me about GUHS. They served a delicious hot lunch—like Sunday dinner— roast beef with rich brown gravy over creamy, mashed potatoes, green beans, and fresh bread, which I loved.

Second, the sophomore year English class was devoted to reading and analyzing poetry in infinite detail. I could see no need for this, although Edgar Allan Poe seemed to fit right in with the manacing insane asylum with its dark, empty windows. "Nevermore!"

The third thing flabbergasted me! I thought I was a sophisticated city girl and here the seniors ran around at the end of the school year squirting each other with water pistols and talking of watermelon busts. They also spoke disparagingly of Californians who would rob them of their water. It was the first I had heard of the controversy.

I didn't find a friend for the summer, so I walked a lot and made watercolor paintings of the stable and cow pasture. The following year, I took the city bus and rode seven miles the other direction into downtown to attend Phoenix Technical School as a commercial art major. I was delighted with the three hours of art shop every day, two solid subjects, and no required physical education. The teachers were charming, intelligent human beings and my attitude and grades prospered.

Many of the boys were in R.O.T.C., and the Tech Drill Team enhanced outdoor ceremonies with shiny chrome helmets, white gloves, and rapid twirling weapons. At indoor occasions, three student country musicians entertained with guitar, fiddle, and steel guitar. Rock-and-roll had not yet been born. Phoenix Tech had great school spirit which helped our baseball, football, and basketball teams. Even though we were a small school, our boys won All City/All State Championships and were so elated they threw the coach in the shower in his new worsted wool suit!

The year after my graduation in 1953, I enrolled at Arizona State College to continue my art studies under Tom J. Harter. Our life-drawing models were fellow students wearing bathing suits or P. E. shorts. How times have changed.

---

*Lois D. McCarty Banks now lives in Phoenix.*

# Glimpses: 1940-59

## BROWNMOOR SCHOOL FOR GIRLS – AND HORSES
### Bea Barlow Costa

In September of 1944 after a hot two-day trip from California, I arrived at Brownmoor School for girls. It was founded by Miss Mary Moore and Miss Justine Browne, who had bought a defunct resort on Indian School Road. The school moved into it after losing its lease at Bishop's lodge in Santa Fe, New Mexico. There were neat, little bungalows with screened porches where we would sleep on hot nights—no air conditioning! Large olive trees graced the grounds, also a swimming pool, tennis courts, and stables for the horses. I always took my horse to school. He arrived by train to be ridden to the stables by our resident cowboy, a man we called Oat.

The school was mainly for boarders, but we had several day students. We rode horses to Scottsdale along the canals and tied them up in the dusty streets while we would get a drink of water. We rode past young German prisoners who worked along the roadways and waved to us, calling in broken English, "Hello, Miss Americas."

We exchanged dances with Judson School for Boys and participated in tennis tournaments throughout the state. The top players of each school were invited for exhibition matches at Camelback Inn, the Biltmore, Paradise Inn, and Jokake Inn. We would fill up on the gourmet food and then play. We met Clark Gable, Jimmy Stewart, Joan Caulfield, and June Allyson. They would invite us to join them in a game. We also played Arizona State College. Our Instructor, Miss Boles, was a graduate of the college, and she coached us long and well.

Frank Lloyd Wright was in residence at Taliesin, and we had dances with his students. Some of us attended the Sunday soirees where Mr. Wright spoke. They were held outside, and as the canvas overhangs were not finished when thunderstorms came up the party was over.

Religious services were usually conducted by the Episcopal Bishop Kinsolving, who came Sunday afternoons to deliver his spellbinding sermons. We adored him and he reciprocated.

We were strictly supervised and only allowed to go to town once every four weeks for shopping. One year my roommate, sponsored by Porter's, became rodeo queen much to our joy and the school's dismay. We all went to the rodeo to cheer for her, ate too much junk food, got sick, and promptly were campused for a month. Phoenix had a junior rodeo, and a couple of girls entered unbeknownst to the school. Again we were campused and the culprits almost sent home, only to be saved through the persuasiveness of Oat, our friend.

We had an excellent academic education which easily carried those who chose on to college. The school tried hard to make ladies of us, and most of us did grow up, marry, and have families. Through the years we have maintained our close friendships with one another.

*Bea Barlow Costa now lives in Scottsdale.*

## A TEACHER WITH MISSIONARY ZEAL
### Arturo Rosales

My family lived in Amado in the 1940s and early '50s. We owe a debt of thanks to Mrs. Mary Martin, who although she was a public school teacher, had a missionary zeal for her job. She was a widow and lived in a mobile home with another teacher. They devoted their whole lives to teaching.

When my two older sisters graduated from elementary school, the county provided a bus that they could have ridden for thirty miles into Nogales High School, but my parents were hesitant about it, especially my dad. He didn't like the fact that everyone had to take physical education and the girls had to wear shorts. So my sisters didn't go to high school, but Mrs. Martin tutored them and gave them books to read, and in general encouraged them to study.

Also, I think it was Mrs. Martin who helped influence my dad to move our family to Eloy so that my sisters could attend high school in a safe environment. Mrs. Martin continued tutoring them when we lived in Eloy, and after two years of course work, they graduated from Santa Cruz Valley Union High School with honors. College was out of the question. You can imagine the stories my dad had heard about girls in college.

It sounds oppressive, huh? Still you have to weigh and balance a number of other factors. We all turned out just fine, and it must be in part because of our upbringing.

*In 1958, the Rosales family moved to Tucson where Arturo finished his schooling. He went on to earn a Ph.D. at Indiana University and is now a professor of history at ASU.*

## AJO MEMORIES
### Bertha Garrison

The first year I taught in Ajo, three boys in my sixth-grade class were the sons of coaches or former coaches. As the World Series was approaching, these boys wanted to bring a radio to school so they could listen to the games. I consented, providing they copy down the assignments in Math and English, complete these assignments as homework, and give them to me for grading before the radio could be turned on.

The boys completed their work in record time. When it was time for the game to begin, the radio was brought in. At the back of the room, they laid flat on their stomachs radiating out from the radio like spokes on a wheel. They had charts for each team and were keeping statistics and figuring averages, etc. The rest of the class were at their desks carrying on with their usual classroom activities.

Unexpectedly the superintendent of the Ajo Schools came into the room. Mr. Dicus was a former coach at Jerome and Bisbee High Schools and the father of one of the boys on the floor. He looked at this scene for a moment and started to walk out of the room. I rushed after him to try to explain what was going on and why. He just said, "I like that."

Another memory I have is of Adolfo, a big overgrown boy in the sixth grade, who had a great deal of difficulty with math. While the rest of the class worked on their assignments, I would try to help Adolfo. Maria, sitting across the aisle from Adolfo, had the hiccoughs. I finally told her to go to the water fountain and get a drink. The hiccoughs continued. To my surprise, Adolfo suddenly shouted "Maria, I saw you steal Tony's pencil."

"I did not steal Tony's pencil."

"Yes you did. I saw you."

"I did not," and Maria began crying.

"See," said Adolfo, "I made you mad and stopped your hiccoughs. I ain't so dumb."

*Bertha Garrison is now retired after 43 years of teaching in Clarkdale and Ajo.*

## CAMPUS PATRIOTISM
### Dorothy Robinson

World War II was hard on the State Teachers College. We lost students and faculty until barely 2,000 were on campus. In the training school, we had a Junior Red Cross program, gardens, drives, and other activities connected with the war effort. I helped with the Red Cross in the training school and college. One year we made Christmas decorations for the German prisoner-of-war camp in Papago Park. The year before, a number of prisoners had escaped one night during a storm by tunneling under the fence. I believe they were all captured. Until that news was verified, we were vaguely uneasy.

Corps of student officers were trained on campus. The boys in uniform swinging along in time to their songs were exciting and gave us a feeling of being in things. "Pistol Packin' Mama" was a favorite. Because of war conditions, there was a lack of teachers. One year I taught geography to the cadets for a few weeks.

*Dorothy Robinson was librarian at the training school in Tempe.*

## MOVING TO THE CITY
### Lorenzo Rhoton

In 1943, I applied to be a principal in Lehi outside of Mesa. I think I got the job because the School Board was impressed that as principal in Taylor I had already started a federally supported, hot lunch program; at least that was what they talked the most about in the interview. They never even asked about my schooling. I was glad because I did not earn my bachelor's degree until 1946, a full 33 years after I began teaching.

The Taylor lunch program that the Lehi people were impressed with cost the children ten cents a day. Grownups had to pay more. My sister and her husband, who were fine old southern cooks, prepared the food. It was common for townspeople, who had no place else to eat out, to stop by the school for lunch. The way it worked was that the federal government provided certain commodities and some money. The rest came from the children and the grownups who ate the lunches.

When I moved to Lehi, we began a similar program, but in Lehi the cooks would stop by the local produce sheds where the managers would save discards for them. We had such fresh, delicious salads that when I went through the cafeteria line I always turned my plate around so that in the big partition I got salad and in the little one I got beans.

Moving from Taylor to Mesa was an adjustment for my wife and our five children. In Mesa, there were different schools for different grade levels. On the first day of school we accompanied the younger children, but our oldest daughter, who was in sixth grade, went by herself. She was given some kind of a task which she did not succeed in, and was therefore put in the lowest level class. She had always been at the top of her class and was mortified to be identified as a poor student. As the days went by, she grew more and more unhappy, especially since there was another girl in the school who had moved from Taylor and would have nothing to do with anyone in the low section. The teacher telephoned to tell us that our daughter did not belong in this section. We asked the teacher to get her transferred, but she did not dare approach the principal since making the assignments was considered to be in his domain.

I had troubles enough being principal of a new school, and so I didn't worry about the matter as much as my wife did. Then one day I came home to find my daughter crying and my wife announcing that if I didn't do something about the matter she was taking her children and moving back to Taylor. I did not want to interfere with the way another principal ran his school, but neither did I want my wife and children to leave, so I approached the principal. He reluctantly agreed to let my daughter try a class one section higher: "But if she doesn't make it, she'll have to go right back." I said I couldn't ask for more. The matter turned out all right, and as the months went by my daughter was gradually moved up and up. Each time she was promoted, I would remind her of how important it was to remain friends with the kids in the section she was leaving, but I'm not sure my chiding had any effect.

I never thought this kind of grouping was good for education. Throughout more than fifty years as a teacher, my philosophy was always that happy kids learn better and that happy teachers do better jobs. Categorizing kids works against this kind of happiness.

*Lorenzo Rhoton retired from the Mesa Public Schools in 1967 and now lives in Mesa.*

## ATTENDING EVERY SCHOOL IN TEMPE
## Jane Hilgeman Sanderson

I started school at the top by going to nursery school and kindergarten on the Arizona State College campus. I remember Miss Kagy's kind face and caring hugs, the guinea pigs, the playground, and in kindergarten the wide steps that were fun to run up and down, sit on, and play on. Those wide steps and my kindergarten building are no longer part of the campus, but my nursery school building is now the Center for Family Studies.

I didn't really want to be in school because it restricted the freedom I was used to. In 1951, I began first grade at Ritter, one of the first schools in Tempe. My family lived five miles south of Tempe in the Rural School District, but my parents thought the Tempe schools were better and so they paid tuition for my brother and me. The teacher was stern, hitting our knuckles with a ruler if we didn't give a correct answer. The principal seemed equally stern. My poor mother must have gotten some of her grey hair that year because I cried my way to school each day.

The next year, Tempe had built Mitchell School on the west side of town, and we were in its boundaries. Here in the second grade, Miss Tyler, who was soft spoken and gentle, made learning fun. She used games to teach math and spelling, and we gathered in small groups to read from *Dick and Jane*, but the bus rides were terrible.

Coming in the morning wasn't too bad because I was one of the last to be picked up. I lived on what is now Priest between Southern and Baseline. We went as far east as Price Road and as far south as Ray Road then along Baseline with detours down McClintock and Canal Drive (Rural Road). My bus stop was at Baseline and Priest from which I walked the final quarter of a mile. I would get out of school at 2:00 p.m. and arrive home about 4:30.

Tempe was growing fast, and the District built another school. Again the boundaries changed and I attended Broadmor School for fifth and sixth grades.

With my new bus schedule, I would now arrive about 7:00 a.m. We were supposed to stay on the playground until school started, but I made friends with Miss Virginia Brady, one of the first grade teachers, and I soon spent most of my early mornings helping her. That friendship is still intact, and we see each other at least once a year, even though she now lives in New Mexico. The most memorable part of the next year was when all the sixth grade classes merged into one group and Mrs. Windes, taught us to square dance.

The school boundaries changed again and so the next year I went to the old Tenth Street Grammar School. I only got to stay there for half of the seventh grade, but it was my favorite of all the school buildings. The library was huge and had hardwood floors and big windows along the north side. There were, of course, rows of bookshelves and long reading tables but the room was light and airy. This was the only school with an auditorium. Once they had a carnival that took up most of the lawn in front of the school.

One of the games was a ring toss, and the prize was a live duck, which my brother won. I don't remember how we got the duck home, but I do remember that mother was less-than-pleased.

There were plays and musicals in the auditorium. The floor was hardwood and red velvet curtains hung in front while others could be let down at different places on stage. Dressing rooms were under the stage in a basement area. Mrs. Wochner, our music teacher, put on a Christmas program, and I got to stand on the auditorium stage and sing. Then there were dance lessons in the cafeteria one afternoon a week. After we had been taught to dance all fall, the school had a Christmas party. It was my first formal dance.

In mid-year, Tempe's first junior high was finished. Shortly after Christmas we moved into McKemy School. We kept our same system of one teacher except for art, music, and library, but the next year we had a home room teacher with separate teachers for math, home economics, and music. Our music teacher organized the Triple Trio and Blue Boys, two groups who gave performances around the community as well as programs at school.

My eighth grade graduation was held on the lawn of Broadmor School. I don't know why it wasn't held at McKemy—perhaps because there wasn't much grass on the new playground. My mother had always sewed my clothes, but for this momentous occasion I had my first "boughten" dress.

I seemed to have followed new schools as they were built in Tempe, but when I got to Tempe High School in 1959 it had been there long enough for not only grass but trees to grow. My real memories of Tempe High are tied in with the U.D.I. (University Drive-In), a hamburger stand at the corner of Rural Road and Apache Boulevard. It was as much a part of high school as if it had been on the campus. That was where we went to discuss teachers, home work, boys, cars, and who was going with whom over a cherry coke and the best hamburgers I've ever eaten.

*Jane Hilgeman Sanderson works in the Graduate College at Arizona State University a short walk from where she began nursery school.*

## NAILS IN THE ROAD
### Helen Kolbe

When we moved to Patagonia, in 1948, the total high school budget was $17,000 for a year. This had to pay the three teachers' salaries, building maintenance, supplies, buses, etc. One teacher had her master's degree from ASU and her salary was $4,000. When the other teachers' salaries were paid, there wasn't a lot left. There were about 85 students, and classes were held in a warehouse. The town heard that the surplus barracks from Ft. Huachuca were being sold for $50.00 each, plus moving costs.

Patagonia bought a few of these barracks and was able to build a high school at a very reasonable cost. Those barracks went to schools all over the state, some going to the college in Tempe to be used as married student housing. The road between Sonoita and Tucson, which today is Interstate 10 but then was called Benson highway, was closed two mornings a week—I think it was Wednesday and Friday—so the barracks could be moved. We hated to travel on this gravel highway because we would get flat tires from the nails that shook out of the bouncing buildings.

*Helen Kolbe now lives at Friendship Village in Mesa, Arizona*

## PIGEON DROPPINGS AND RELATED CONSIDERATIONS
### Duane Manning

Editor's Note: *While gathering stories for this history, one thing we learned is that there's no end to the variation in the problems faced by educators. And, like the problem described in the memo below, most can be solved only partially. It was written when all education classes and offices met on the central campus in Old Main.*

Old Main on the ASU campus in 1954. *Arizona State University Archives photo.*

TO: Arizona State Elementary Education Faculty Members

FROM: Duane Manning, Department Chairman

SUBJECT: Pigeon Droppings and Related Considerations

DATE: September 17, 1953

One of the major unsolved problems confronting the College as we move into the year is the problem of pigeon droppings. There is a grave urgency about this matter and we have not attacked it with our customary vigor and legislative activity.

The solution remains a dilemma. Some faculty members go around to the north door, but this is running away from the problem and seems a cowardly way out. Others have resorted to a verbal approach bad-mouthing the pigeons in the sanctity of their offices—a dangerous technique for pigeons are sensitive to personal abuse and are very delicately triggered. We must look for better ways.

I do not wish to be discouraging. We are daily picking up new advocates for action. Ralston was struck only yesterday and is now urging a militant program. Until then he had insisted it was simply a problem in semantics. There is some encouragement also in Ashe's survey which reveals only one chance in five of being hit on any given trip. This is due to the habits of pigeons which cause them to intersperse activity with occasional periods of rest. We dare not use this, however, as justification for relaxing or delaying action. We must develop a bold and imaginative approach.

We may assume our faculty will be divided on the proper approach. Wochner favors détente while Baker urges massive retaliation. The latter may be fraught with danger since the College of Education constitution did not anticipate this eventuality, nor define a modus operandi.

Dean McGrath should initiate the project by reviewing individual variation in pigeon's productivity. Schall may interrupt excitedly to point out that each has done his mite and deserves an "A." Heimann will review the research to prove that, all our experience notwithstanding, you cannot tell a diarrheic pigeon from the other kind. I can hear Jelinek saying gravely . . . "This poses a real problem."

Davis may question the purpose of our pigeon project. We will assure him that we seek in no way to block the pigeons' constitutional processes. Podlich is likely to raise an issue about the rights of the minorities, but surely the evidence that piles up at our West entrance is not the work of a minority.

It is obvious that this problem requires our best thinking. To assist in this reflective activity, I have summarized the more pertinent facts:

1. Pigeon droppings are almost always caused by pigeons. This is one of our most basic ideas. I hope you will appreciate the lucid manner in which it is stated. There is one exception to this, however. Droppings do somehow seem to appear during faculty and committee meetings. This phenomenon has never been satisfactorily explained.
2. Pigeon droppings tend almost invariably toward extremes. Some splatter. Others are dry and may be easily crushed between the thumb and forefinger. In a paper of this size I simply do not have time to go into the reasons for this.
3. Pigeons do have other interests. Although they specialize in the activity which has created our dilemma, they also court, mate, and reproduce other pigeons. This increases the total droppings. I hope I have not been too candid in explaining this.

On a final note I should like to state for the record that we are a peace loving group and did not seek this squalid little confrontation. It was thrust upon us. But now that the battle is joined, let us rise magnificently to the cause and teach these reckless aggressors that they cannot with impunity soil and degrade the quality of our lives.

We can and must achieve victory. Then in the larger arena of life let us vow to relentlessly pursue and eradicate droppings in whatever form whenever and wherever they may appear. This is our mission and may well be our ultimate destiny.

*Duane Manning was the first chair of the Department of Elementary Education at Arizona State College. His more serious writings include* The Qualitative Elementary School *and* Toward a Humanistic Curriculum *published by Harper and Row.*

## FACTS FROM THE BOOK CLOSET
## Jim Hartdegen

I was raised in Eloy where I attended both elementary and high school. I have many fond memories of school, but would like to tell you about a teacher I had in seventh grade. For obvious reasons, I will refer to him only as Mr. F. Many times Mr. F. would come to class in a sweat, with shaking hands, and on occasions he could not make it through the day without lying down in the book closet. One day when he was out of the room, we examined the closet and found a whiskey bottle behind some books on the top shelf and mouth wash on the bottom shelf. Despite Mr. F.'s problem, I would say my class did very well.

*Jim Hartdegen now lives in Casa Grande and is a member of the Arizona House of Representatives.*

## SCHOOL IN CORNVILLE
## Candy E. Terry

When I started first grade in 1955, my school in Cornville (Oak Creek), Arizona, was a little red one-room schoolhouse with the traditional bell on top. It was only about two miles from our home, but it was on the other side of a creek and there was no crossing. We actually lived between two creeks—Oak Creek and Spring Creek—so there were some days during spring floods when we were stranded at home and couldn't go to school. There were also a few days when we were stranded at school and couldn't get home.

At first my father and mother helped me wade across Oak Creek so I could climb the hill to the paved road where the school bus came. It was about a 3/4-mile walk. After school I sometimes played with friends who lived by the bus stop until my mother could wade over to get me. Later we discovered I could get off the bus at another place, cross the creek on a swinging bridge, and walk about a mile home. One day I dawdled on the swinging bridge trying to catch fish. My mother was out of her mind worrying about me. I never dawdled again!

The one room of the school could be used either as an auditorium, or as separate classrooms by the two teachers who each taught three grades. I was amazed at how they could divide the room by pulling out a wall made of wooden slats.

Recesses were spent crawling under the steps that led up to the door or playing out in the rocky, dry terrain around the schoolhouse. I don't remember any playground fences or limits, but nobody wandered too far away. There were tales of mountain lions in the surrounding hills.

In the middle of that first year, we moved out of this little red schoolhouse and into the new brick building across the dirt road. It had two rooms *and* a big separate auditorium with a stage at one end. We were very

*Oak Creek School District photo.*

excited as we carried stacks of dusty books to the new rooms which we had never seen before. New desks were waiting for us in six neat, little rows (two rows per grade level).

A few years later my father routed out a big sign, "Oak Creek School," for the front of the building. The sign that is there today looks like it might be the same one. The bell on top of the school looks the same too. It must have been moved over from the little red schoolhouse.

One winter morning my brother was the talk of the school when he broke a frozen hose into pieces. Mr. Preston, the new man teacher, swatted him several times with a piece of the hose.

Mr. Preston somehow taught me to love to diagram sentences, and to love poetry. I still remember the poem, "School Days" by John Greenleaf Whittier, probably because it made me think of a romanticized version of my little old one-room school.

> Still sits the schoolhouse by the road,
> A ragged beggar sleeping;
> Around it still the sumachs grow,
> And blackberry-vines are creeping . . . .

Actually, the old school had been torn down and there were never any blackberry vines. It was so dry that getting anything to grow was a challenge. We were taught to be very careful with all plants. A special treat was to play on the school's front lawn during Friday afternoon recess. We didn't dare step on it at any other time.

School was the center for everything that went on in the community. People voted in the auditorium, and the Homemakers' Club met there during school. After school, the 4-H club used it. It was the place for community potlucks, dances, little theater performances, seasonal parties, school programs, and Little League practices.

During school hours, ringing the bell hanging above the breezeway was one of the honors bestowed upon deserving children, so at night we loved to jump up and catch the bell's big rough rope and pull with all our might. The best part was being scared by the bats that would fly out. Now I find it strange that no one took steps to get rid of those bats!

*Candy E. Terry went on to become a teacher and is now earning her master's degree at ASU.*

## AN INTERVIEW WITH MARJORIE ENTZ
### Kim Rutherford

"Whatever you work hardest at, you'll love the most. If something comes easy, you won't appreciate it," says Marjorie Entz, a former physical education teacher and coach at Mesa High School. Miss Entz graduated from Mesa High in 1924; then after college returned to her alma mater where she taught for 36 years. She is best remembered for her dedicated work with the Rabbettes, a girls' group of marchers, flag twirlers, and rope twirlers that performed with the Jackrabbit band during halftime at football games and eventually expanded into doing parades and other special shows. They became famous throughout Arizona because of their flair for putting on a show.

The Rabbettes started as a pep-club in 1925 to supplement the championship basketball team of that year. Originally, they were El Connettes (the Jackrabbits with a female touch), then the Peppettes, the elite girls' club on campus. After a decade, Miss Entz took control of the Peppettes and made them into an actual class, one that performed with the band. They wore saddle shoes, white skirts, purple and gold reversible bolero vests, and beanies. In 1948, a vote was called for, and Rabbettes became the official name.

With a new Western look in 1953, the Rabbettes became better known throughout the state. "We became famous because we were so different," Miss Entz explained. "Nowadays every band has flags and rifles, but back then hardly anyone had flags, and no one had ropers except Mesa High."

She has fond memories of her days with the Rabbettes and keeps four scrapbooks bursting with Mesa High history. One year there were 113 members. "It got out of hand—it was crazy but a lot of fun." Then, during World War II, shoes were rationed. "We'd always worn high quality boots and now had to construct fake boots out of white oilcloth. The girls hated them because they fell off a lot."

One of Miss Entz's proudest memories is of the last half-time show she sponsored. "I knew that last show they were up to something secret. During the halftime, the band started playing 'Margie,' and they spelled ENTZ in huge letters across the playing field. Then the leader of the Rabbettes presented me with 36 roses, one for each year at Mesa High."

When Marjorie Entz retired, the Rabbettes became history because no one wanted to put in the work to keep them going. They have been replaced by the Color Guard and the Bunnies pom line.

*Kim Rutherford is a student at Mesa High School.*

# 1960-1985: Accomplishments and Challenges

The 1960-85 period is one of both accomplishments and challenges. Newcomers continued to move into the state and to suffer culture-shock when their children came home from school covered with mud from playing "irrigation soccer" or covered with bandages because of getting burned on solar-heated playground equipment.

In 1960, there were 615 Arizona public schools; in 1970 the number was 757, while in 1980 it was 861. Learning pods, open classrooms, and team teaching were some of the ways that schools tried coping with an ever-changing population. Alternatives to traditional public schooling proliferated. The 1960-61 report of the state superintendent listed 22 private schools. A decade later, it listed 142, and still a decade later it listed 484, approximately half of which were pre-schools or kindergartens. Year-round schooling appeared on the horizon with summer schools being offered for enrichment as well as remediation. Fifteen cities and towns now have community colleges. Adult and juvenile correctional institutions established in-house education programs. Adults taking the GED test of high school equivalency increased from 1,604 in 1960-61 to over 8,000 in 1983-84. Larger districts have special schools or programs for teenage mothers, for children whose parents want them to have a "basic" education, for children with behavioral and emotional problems, and for gifted students.

One of the biggest changes that took place between 1960 and 1985 was an increased reliance of local school districts on federal monies. Such funding in 1960-61 was negligible, mostly supporting districts near military bases or with Indian children. Ten years later, the 1970-71 state superintendent's report showed 39 million federal dollars received by Arizona districts, while a decade later the figure was 142 million dollars. These funds were first used to help school libraries acquire science and math books. Areas later receiving heavy support were reading, and special, vocational, bilingual, and early childhood education, particularly for the culturally disadvantaged. The Civil Rights Act of 1965 tied federal funding in with a mechanism through which parents, students, and school employees could file grievances if they thought they were being discriminated against because of race or sex.

This provided grounds for some of the controversies of the period. Complainants felt hampered by red tape and time delays. On the other side, school officials felt the procedures assumed guilt until innocence was proven. Book selection was another controversy. The tiny town of St. David received nationwide publicity when the school board voted to ban John Steinbeck's *Of Mice and Men* from the high school.

Legislative decisions of the period include the 1965 reorganization of the State Board of Education, a plan to purchase high school textbooks for needy students, a requirement that teachers pass a basic-skills competency test prior to certification, the granting of state support for half-day kindergartens, and the establishment of mandatory schooling through tenth grade.

Since writing about this period is a matter of making current social observations, we asked a sampling of knowledgeable Arizonans to describe either a significant achievement made in Arizona schools within the last 25 years or a challenge facing these schools in the next 25 years.

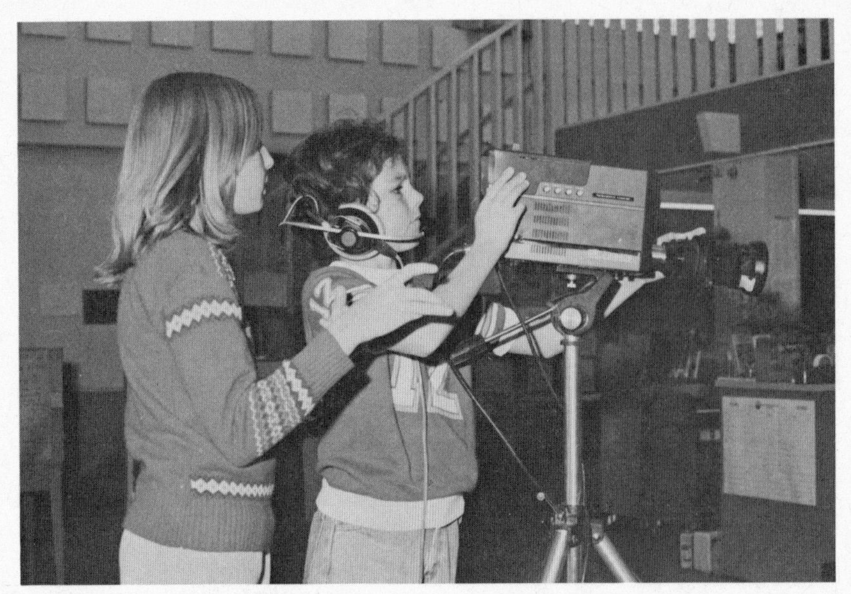

Longfellow School in Mesa, 1982.

Sacaton First Grade, 1984.

Signs of the times, Tempe, 1985.

Payne Training School at ASU, 1963.

**Congressman Eldon Rudd, Scottsdale**
**Arizona Representative, Fourth District**

The National Commission on Excellence in Education startled the country with its 1983 report on the state of education and reawakened nationwide interest and concern for the improvement of public schools across the land. The Nation—Arizona in particular—responded with reforms to ensure a better education for our children and, in turn, a stronger economy, more productive community, and better security for us all. Those reforms include changes in curriculum for elementary and secondary school students, increased graduation requirements for high school students, raised admissions requirements for the state's universities, a greater number of days in the school year, and incentives for students to pursue math and science at the college level.

As one who believes that states, rather than the federal government, should maintain primary authority over education, I applaud these efforts. I think our greatest challenge for the future is to keep federal bureaucrats on the sidelines while we encourage higher standards and accept the challenge of keeping education in the forefront of community concern.

**Roy Doyle, Tempe**
**Teacher Educator**

Arizona's public schools in the past half century have awakened to the range of individual differences among children and the responsibility to accommodate these differences. This less restricted view of human educability brings to light some invisible problems of the past which remain our greatest challenge of the future.

I graduated from Glendale Grammar School in 1935, and I am now struck by how few of my classmates from Spanish speaking homes entered and persisted through Glendale Union High School. Academic standards were high, and it was not uncommon for a student to fail English twice before losing hope of graduation. The schools operated under the comfortable assumption that it was the students and not the schools who were failing. The success of schools was measured in terms of the abilities of the graduates, with little recognition of the filtering system which conveniently separated the "educable" from the "uneducable."

During the past quarter century, changes in the student population of Arizona's public schools have accelerated. Native Americans, formerly educated by the Bureau of Indian Affairs, have entered the public schools in record numbers, and other racial and ethnic minorities have been encouraged to persist longer in their education. Our schools were never as successful with these children as with those from families with a tradition of education and a commitment to intellectual pursuits. The proportion of children from this latter type of family has decreased sharply because of the declining birth rate at the upper socio-economic levels—the levels at which schools have always had their most spectacular success.

The greatest challenge facing Arizona's schools lies in finding better ways to meet the educational needs of those children not inclined toward education as we have traditionally presented it. We must learn to serve students with contrasting backgrounds and aspirations and find better ways to assess a wider range of student accomplishment.

**Representative Jim Cooper, Mesa**
**Chair, House Education Committee**

Arizona has met the challenge of making quality education available to all school-age children. Our vocational programs and our programs for handicapped students far exceed the national average. Now we must see that the universities upgrade their Colleges of Education so that we will have capable, qualified teachers.

**Dorothy L. Bray, Casa Grande**
**Teacher/Administrator**

When I began teaching at Casa Grande Junior High School in 1962, a student could be punished for speaking any language other than English—even during recess or lunch breaks. I'm happy that through teacher training in linguistics and special education, for example, the system has become more humanized, and students, parents, teachers, and administrators now recognize that we live in a multicultural, mobile world where we can accept the languages and values of others without giving up our own.

**Susie O'Connor, Ajo**
**Retired Teacher**

When I began teaching in Ajo in 1940, all classes were racially segregated, one section for "whites" and another for Mexicans and Indians. Every aspect of the community was also segregated: churches, swimming pool, park, and neighborhoods. In 1948, classes were integrated and shortly thereafter segregation was nonexistent in the community. The change was not all swift and serene, but it did come about, and the schools deserve to be commended for the part they played.

**Donald G. Shropshire, Tucson**
**Taxpayer**
The biggest accomplishment of the past 25 years was the adoption of Chapter 119 by the Arizona Legislature which in 1960 authorized the community college system.

**Yetta Goodman, Tucson**
**Professor of Education**
In 1976 a statewide committee for the Arizona Young Readers' Award and Arizona Young Authors' Conferences was formed. Its purpose was to encourage reading and writing among the young people of Arizona. Teachers, librarians, book sellers, authors, and parents can be proud of their work on this committee. Emphasis alternates between reading and writing, with conferences held each spring both at the University of Arizona and Arizona State University. In the reading years, students vote from a list of twenty for a favorite book. They must read at least five books from the list before they vote. In the most recent contest, over 33,000 students voted, which means that a minimum of 165,000 books were read, mostly outside of class. Winning authors, including Judy Blume and Thomas Rockwell, have come to Arizona to receive their awards and to interact with young readers.

Similar large numbers of young people have written their own books for local young-author conferences where they share their stories with each other and appreciative parents. Representatives then attend the state-wide conferences at ASU and the U of A. Widely published authors who have come to share professional advice with young writers include Jean George, Tomie de Paola, Bill Martin, Jr., Jack Prelutsky, and Alvin Schwartz.

**Juanita Harelson, Tempe**
**State Senator**
Rewarding "master teachers" with higher pay as former Secretary of Education Terrell Bell suggested, will increase the attractiveness of the profession, but such a financial incentive won't keep teachers from leaving if they must suffer through the frustrations of mandates, rules and regulations, administrators' arbitrary behavior, and lack of parental concern. Another challenge we must meet is to achieve comprehensive curricula by paying careful attention to the use of time, and placing a high premium on independent thinking.

**George N. Smith, Flagstaff**
**NAU Vice President and Executive Director,**
**Center for Excellence in Education**
The most important challenge facing Arizona's educational system is to respond successfully to rapid change. As educators, we have to assume an assertive posture of anticipation and preparedness, especially at local levels, as we work to understand how the following forces will affect education.

> Schools must keep up with the information explosion which quickens the pace of change and makes it that much harder for schools to be recognized, understood, and supported as the foundation of economic progress and national well being.
>
> As Arizona becomes one of the key technological centers of the nation, our schools will have to produce graduates better prepared for employment. If we fail, business, industry, and other agencies will assume the educational role.
>
> The shift to the sun belt will bring an increasing number of senior citizens who are interested in life-long learning programs and activities.
>
> Dramatic changes in life styles will result in more one-parent familes and "latchkey" children who will have to be served.
>
> The increase in leisure activities and the related industries of recreation and travel will demand new educational programs.
>
> Educational counseling programs will have to emphasize a preventive, guidance approach as opposed to remediating students' needs.
>
> Improved programs and preventive strategies must be used to reduce the student dropout rate.
>
> As an economic necessity, educators will have to make more efficient use of school facilties and apply greater expertise in reducing operations, maintenance, and energy costs.
>
> To establish and maintain an adequate support base, educators must inform the general public about the financial and social realities of education. Policy makers will have to become more knowledgeable, rather than more political, in their decision-making responsibilities.

To meet these challenges, I believe we must emphasize the following five points:

> *Identify* only high quality people as potential educators.
>
> *Recruit* only high quality people into education.
>
> *Provide* only high quality *Preparation* programs
>
> *Place* outstanding people in our educational system.
>
> *Maintain* our educational system in such a fashion as to *Retain* only high quality people.

**Sam and Ruth Cooper, Tucson**
**Teachers/Administrators**
As a society which has pledged its support to an educated populace, we stand almost alone. Much has been accomplished, but much remains to challenge us. While living in an area approaching a 40 percent minority population, our public university has a minority population of less than three percent. Twenty miles from a downtown metropolis, children on reservations are hampered by educational shortcomings. We hotly debate bilingual education while countless children languish in classes they do not understand. Although a rallying cry for over a decade, *mainstreaming* of the handicapped remains a dirty word. Hundreds of migrant students are shuffled in and out of systems which cannot or will not respond to their needs. Far too many public schools remain inaccessible to the physically handicapped; major funding discrepancies still exist between metropolitan and rural districts, and the dropout rate is alarming, cutting students off from the society most of us take for granted.

Our mission lest we forget in the day-to-day grind and frustration, is almost a sacred one. We are very special people doing a very special task. No one can afford for us to fail.

**Willard Abraham, Tempe**
**University Professor**
We have made a significant start, but we have a long way to go in educating our gifted children. Among common misunderstandings are the following:

Gifted children "ripen" early (intellectually) and "rot" early (emotionally).

They are so bright that they can manage to get through school without counseling.

It is undemocratic to single them out in any way.

They are eccentric, kind of peculiar, and have more than their share of health problems and difficulties in being with other people.

We have to wait until past early childhood before we can identify them as being gifted.

All of these statements are false. The truths about bright children need to be brought to the attention of educators and the public. It won't be the intellectually less-than-gifted who will solve the problems of nuclear energy, war, cancer, poverty, and over-population. Educating our gifted youngsters to their capacities is essential for survival. Such a statement is not a simplistic conclusion, but rather a description of a complex and demanding task which will require insightful leadership from all elements of our society.

**Barbara and William D. Searle, Scottsdale**
**Librarian and Taxpayers**
The challenges facing Arizona schools are similar to those facing the rest of the nation, only more so, due to the rapid growth of our state and our cultural and vocational diversity. We provide some of the best education in the world for students raised under favorable circumstances but only mediocre education for large numbers of young people with average or low motivation. The magnitude of the problem is borne out by achievement test results and by the menacing growth of an underclass of young unemployables and functional illiterates. Schools must note these serious symptoms and the more conservative and results-oriented mood of the country. They must restore confidence in their programs through showing greater academic emphasis and higher standards of performance at one end of the spectrum, and more remedial education and job-oriented training at the other. And this must be accomplished in a more cost-effective manner than in the past. That's about as big a challenge as one could find!

Public schools with their entrenched bureaucracies and over-regulation and political pressures— internal and external from both the left and the right—may not be capable of accommodating these demands. But if private schools are to become the badly-needed educational change agents which will provide needed competition for the public schools, they too must become more flexible and innovative —particularly in the areas of finance and fund raising. They must learn to accommodate cultural and intellectual diversity, and fundamentalist religious schools and others with a special interest orientation must achieve a balance of viewpoints and subject matter without compromising in the pursuit of truth—wherever it may lead.

**Roy M. Claridge, Tucson**
**Teacher Educator**
Our greatest challenge is to plan ahead for the influx of people predicted to arrive in Arizona within the next 25 years. As Edward C. Simmons said, "The difference between failure and success is doing a thing nearly right and doing it exactly right." The four major teacher training programs in the state currently prepare only 30 percent of new Arizona teachers. Unless we reverse this trend, the population increase will mean that we

will have to bring in more and more people trained in institutions over which we have no control. The shortage of qualified teachers in rural districts is already critical where teachers not prepared in new subject areas are being pressed into service. Resources for teacher training programs have been cut back when they should have been increased. Our children will not have the educational opportunities we have had unless we take steps now to do things "exactly right."

**Jeannette Veatch, Mesa**
**Teacher Educator**

Early childhood education needs to be expanded. Not until 1972 did kindergartens receive state support. It is still only for part-time kindergartens and is given grudgingly. Pre-schools are considered worthy of federal entitlements, but not state support. Financing of day-care centers would have a marked effect on the ability of the working poor to get off welfare rolls.

Connections between liberal arts offerings and teacher preparation curricula need to be made more obvious so that teachers will promote liberal arts values throughout the schooling of children. Also public schools must restore faith in human interactions. Teachers teach. Books and machines do not. We need to reduce our dependence on commercial texts, particularly the fill-in-the-blank type of workbook, and the other mechanistic barbarities of recent years, which work against putting our attention where it belongs—on the relationship between the teacher and the child.

**Gilbert Garcia, Phoenix**
**Consultant to Schools**

Despite shrinking resources, learning opportunities must be provided for Americans of all ages so that they can acquire the knowledge and skills essential for independent living in our complex, highly technological society.

**Betty B. Whetton, Tempe**
**Teacher**

The immediate past has provided teachers with a wealth of information about learners in all their diversities as well as commonalities. We are, therefore, better equipped to teach America's/Arizona's children in the mass while respecting individual needs and problems. The next decades must be devoted to providing better educated teachers. Above all others, elementary teachers need a broadly based education since they are expected to teach all subjects. These changes should include those who aspire to principalships or consultant and administrative posts. A four-year liberal arts education with majors and minors based on interest or aptitude followed by a year of continuing work in education-skills, accompanied by an internship under competent guidance, would soon earn teachers the public respect they now lack and the financial rewards they deserve.

**S. N. Henrie, Prescott**
**Chair of Humanities, Prescott College**

Human society is undergoing a fundamental change as we move from the Industrial Era into the twenty-first century. Science and technology are opening vast, new frontiers of physical existence. Will our emotional, spiritual, social, and intellectual development keep pace? That is the challenge facing Arizona schools.

**Susan Permar, Showlow**
**Teacher**

Yearly, we see an exodus of creative, talented educators who leave to earn more money in business and industry. It isn't that teachers are materialistic, it's that they are finding it increasingly difficult to support familes on such limited incomes. If communities, states, and the country fail to realize that education deserves top priority, the quality of our schools will continue to decline. It's frightening to imagine how low it could go. Let's not find out.

# Reflections on ASU after the Name Change of 1958

G. Homer Durham

When I arrived as president of Arizona State University in September of 1960, the campus was intersected by Tempe City streets. College Avenue (now Cady Mall) was sprinkled with modest dwellings, a barber shop, a small cafe, and a cleaning and dyeing establishment at one end with old Goodwin stadium at the other. Campus buildings were mixed in with stop signs, traffic signals, and moving automobiles. An immediate challenge was the remaking of the physical campus.

A planning unit undertook studies and developed a model. Extraordinary labors by Vice President Gilbert L. Cady and Director of Plant and Planning John R. Ellingson persuaded the City of Tempe to surrender the campus streets. A fountain now stands at the center of what used to be a four-way stop street. The University purchased land east to Rural Road and beyond and north of University Drive so that the old adobe village would no longer separate Sun Devil Stadium from the main campus.

In 1961, funding and final authorization was secured to construct what everyone called the Frank Lloyd Wright auditorium on a different than checkerboard axis. In 1964, when the auditorium was dedicated and named for Grady Gammage, the Philadelphia Orchestra under the direction of Eugene Ormandy made the event special.

However this was just the beginning of the campus-wide development. During the next nine years, some 53 physical facility projects went forward including plans for expanding Sun Devil Stadium first to 50,000 seats and then ultimately to 80,000.

The development of the physical campus was part of a bigger plan of public relations that was a prerequiste to establishing ASU as a major university. Only in November 1958 had our name been changed from *college* to *university*. At the time, Tempe was a small town of some 12,000 people, and I began working to increase our national visibility through identifying ASU as being located "in the heart of the Phoenix Metropolitan area." I also set out to secure membership in the National Association of State Universities and Land Grant Colleges. I was pleased for us to become affiliated with the new Western Athletic Conference because this would bring us to the attention of a national audience who would see us competing with old-line western universities. We also began exploring the possibilities of playing home-and home games with UCLA and other California schools, and in 1968 we saw the birth of the Fiesta Bowl.

Such activities as these are important in building a university because they attract people's attention, but when people begin to look your way, you have to have a faculty and programs worthy of scrutiny. At my first faculty meeting in September of 1960, I said we should aim at making "Tempe as noteworthy a name as Oxford, Cambridge, or Berkeley." Douglas Arner, philosophy professor and chairman of the Faculty Assembly that year, responded that perhaps the new president was a little "over-ambitious." But because of the carry-over of enthusiasm from the recent name-change campaign, many people were ready to join in building a true university. Academic Vice President Harold D. Richardson insisted on excellence. Deans of the four colleges, Arnold Tilden, Guy D. McGrath, Lee P. Thompson, and Glen D. Overman were energetic, capable, and determined to build. Over the next decade, distinguished scholars were recruited. William J. Burke, Gordon B. Castle, and John W. Ryan were brought from older institutions to be vice-presidents. (Ryan later became president of Indiana University.) Charles M. Woolf, who later succeeded Dr. Burke as Vice President for Graduate studies and Dean of the Graduate College, came in 1961. Harry Newburn, past president of the University of Oregon and the University of Montana came in higher education. Inspired by Louis M. Meyers, the Department of English recruited promising young scholars such as Brice Harris and Jerome Archer while Nicholas Salerno and Richard G. Landini flourished in the new environment. Landini went on to become President of Indiana State University.

The institution needed greater strength in the arts and sciences and also more professional schools and colleges. Authorization to grant the Ph.D. in addition to the Ed.D. was essential, and was given in 1961. The College of Engineering was renamed from Applied Arts and Sciences. The colleges of Business, Nursing, Fine Arts, and Architecture all flourished. Under Dean Willard Pedrick the College of Law met its first class in Autumn of 1967 with a new building and a large library. Armstrong Hall was dedicated in 1968 in the presence of U. S. Chief Justice Earl Warren.

Lest, it seem too easy, I should state that we did not achieve all the goals we set. The over-riding issue confronting Arizona universities in 1960 was the establishment of a medical school. ASU desperately wanted to be the home of Arizona's College of Medicine, but in the summer of 1961 the matter was settled in favor of the U of A in Tucson.

The second issue we lost on was much closer to home. Despite the acquisition of land—north, south, east, and west, it was evident that the ASU campus would soon be overgrown. It was already choked on traffic. On May 27, 1966 at commencement, I outlined the desirability of establishing a branch campus.

Regent Arthur B. Schellenberg and ASU Foundation Chairman Charles Wetzler successfully investigated the possibilities of obtaining land for a branch campus at Litchfield Park where the Goodyear Tire and Rubber Company was planning a model city. In July, the Arizona Regents approved my report on the desirability of a branch campus, and Richard G. Landini was named Dean of Litchfield College. His job was to plan the 525 acre campus which the Goodyear Company made available. Caudill, Rowlett, and Scott of Houston, Texas were appointed consulting architects. By early spring of 1969, the physical and academic campus was planned. However, a talented state senator disagreed, and on March 10, 1969 the proposal was crushed at a meeting of a joint legislative committee. The dream was lost to the passions of the era surrounding the Viet Nam war. The land granted by Goodyear had to be given back and the plans laid to rest, not to be reawakened until 12 years later.

Development of a university is a comprehensive team effort. Many forces and groups joined with the faculty and alumni to move ASU ahead following the name change in 1958. I left the presidency in September of 1969 with mixed feelings. President Richard A. Harvill of the University of Arizona later observed that possibly no two presidents in the history of American higher education enjoyed greater support in meeting the needs of a growing state than did the two of us during the 1960s. It was a decade of tremendous building excitement. Today when I return for an occasional visit, it is with deep emotion that I look at the new campus, still developing, but now lined with tree shaded malls instead of city streets. A university de facto greets the Arizona sun each morning.

---

*G. Homer Durham left the presidency at ASU to become Commissioner of Higher Education for the State of Utah.*

# Honor Roll: 1960-1985

| | |
|---|---|
| **Bruce Babbitt** | Seldom has there been an Arizona Governor who gave such a high priority to educational concerns from pre-school through university levels. |
| **Julieta Bencomo** | Bencomo is being honored for being a prime mover in early childhood education, especially through her work as a member and president of the State Board of Education. |
| **Margaret L. Bluhm** | Arizona is a leader in providing schooling for visually handicapped children partially because of the work of Bluhm, who retired in 1981 after serving 13 years as executive director of the Foundation for Blind Children. |
| **William "Bill" Boyle** | Boyle, who served for 25 years in the Tempe School District, most recently as principal of McClintock High School and then as school board member, was nominated because "for many students his caring made the difference." |
| **George Brooks** | In 1963, when Reverend Brooks was elected to the Roosevelt Elementary School Board, he became the first black Arizonan to hold such a position. For over 20 years, he has worked vigorously for equal educational opportunities. |
| **Anthony Chavarria** | In the five years that Chavarria has served as a lay counselor at Marcos de Niza where he works with Indians and some Hispanics, the dropout rate for these students, who make up 25 percent of the district's population, has gone from 40 to less than 10 percent. |
| **Jim Cooper** | Now in his ninth year as Chair of the House Education Committee, Representative Cooper was nominated for his commitment to improving the schooling of all Arizona children. |
| **R. Merwin Deever** | A former school superintendent, Deever joined the ASU faculty in 1959. Besides serving as a professor of educational administration, Deever directed the Bureau of Educational Research and Services and in 1977 was appointed Acting Dean of the College. |
| **Wilburn W. "Skipper" Dick** | As State Superintendent of Public Instruction (1959-65), Dick promoted local control by discontinuing single, statewide textbook adoptions. He also brought unorganized territory into school districts and established accommodation schools in unserved areas. |
| **Sarah Folsom** | Although legislation making kindergartens mandatory was not passed until after her death in 1969, Folsom deserves much of the credit for laying the groundwork that made the change possible. She served as State Superintendent of Public Instruction from 1964-69. |

**Ralph Goitia**

Goitia was nominated for his work in promoting equal educational opportunities for disadvantaged children. While superintendent of the Cottonwood-Oak Creek School District, he helped establish a consortium to set up the first special education classes in the Verde Valley. He served for 14 years on the Title III State Advisory Board, and in 1969 was interim State Superintendent of Public Instruction.

**David Kret**

In the state legislature, Kret spearheaded drives to obtain support for kindergartens and for programs for gifted children.

**Howard "Barney" Leigh**

Between 1969-82, Leigh worked for the improvement of Arizona public schools through his role as the high school visitor for the North Central Accreditation Association.

**Anne Lindemann**

State Senator Lindemann was nominated for her work in support of public schools, especially during the years she served as chair of the Senate Education Committee, 1979-84.

**Leon Maehling**

Maehling served three terms as Yuma County School Superintendent and was also a member of the State Board of Education.

**Harry Newburn**

Newburn came to ASU in 1964 as founding director of the Center of Higher Education. He had been president of the University of Oregon (1945-53) and Montana State University (1959-63), and when Homer Durham resigned in 1969 Newburn was appointed president of ASU.

**Robert F. Paulsen**

A prolific writer on educational theories and issues, Paulsen directed the College of Education at the University of Arizona for 19 years.

**William Payne**

A medical doctor and the son of Ira D. Payne, Bill Payne served on the Tempe School Board for 18 years, as president of the Arizona School Boards Association in 1968, as vice president of the National School Boards Association in 1973, and as a member of the Board of Regents from 1977-84.

**Dix W. Price**

As its first executive director, Price gave leadership to the early growth of the Arizona Education Association. An attorney, he helped draft over 100 education laws and successfully took a school lands case to the Supreme Court making it illegal for a state to take school lands for public use without recompense.

**John Prince**

Prince, who taught for many years in the Phoenix Union High School District, was Chancellor of the Maricopa Community College District during its high growth period in the late '60s and early '70s.

**John Rhodes**

During his quarter of a century in Congress, Rhodes personally welcomed hundreds of young Arizona students to Washington, D.C.: Presidential scholars, 4-H Club or Science Fair winners, delegates to Girls' or Boys' Nation, AFS exchange students, Congressional pages and interns, and on and on and on.

**Norma Richardson**

Richardson retired as superintendent of the Red Mesa School District in 1984. She was the leader charged with creating a new district to meet the needs of a predominantly Navajo population. She was nominated for recruiting an excellent staff, improving the curriculum, and upgrading facilities.

**Robert A. Roessel**

Roessel was nominated for helping to develop the Center for Indian Education at ASU, the Rough Rock Demonstration School, and the Navajo Community College.

**Sister Marijane Ryan**

Sister Marijane Ryan begged and borrowed money, equipment, facilities, and materials to provide programs and hope for handicapped children on the Navajo Reservation as part of St. Michael's School at Window Rock.

**W. P. Shofstall**

State Superintendent of Public Instruction from 1969-74, Shofstall promoted bilingual education, career education, and equal opportunities for minorities.

**George N. Smith**

Former superintendent of Mesa Schools and now Director of the Center for Excellence at NAU, Smith was nominated because he has "set standards of excellence all along the way" and is "one of the few Arizona administrators with measureable national prominence."

**Maria Urquides**

Urquides is a teacher and counselor in Tucson whose longtime support for bilingual education has made an impact at both state and national levels.

**J. Lawrence Walkup**

President of Northern Arizona University from 1957 to 1979, Walkup did much to support teacher education.

**Carolyn Warner**

First elected State Superintendent of Public Instruction in 1974, Warner's administration has been noted for the development of the Arizona Basic Skills Plan; the encouragement of parental participation and partnerships between education, business, industry, and labor, and an efficient use of public funds.

**Morrison P. Warren**

Warren, who served for 15 years as principal of Booker T. Washington School in Phoenix, joined the ASU faculty in 1968. In 1973-74, he took a special leave to be principal of South Mountain High School. He has been on the Phoenix City Council and is now chair of the Arizona Advisory Committee to the United State Commission on Civil Rights.

**John Waters**

Waters began teaching in the Phoenix Union High School District in 1945. He served as principal of Central High School and as Assistant Superintendent for Instruction, and then from 1973 to 1983 as Superintendent of Tempe Union High School District. After his retirement he became a special assistant in the ASU College of Education.

**Delbert D. Weber**

Weber served as Dean of the ASU College of Education during the years of the College's peak enrollments: 1,427 BA degrees in 1973, 114 doctorates in 1974, and 722 master's degrees in 1977. He resigned in 1977 to become Chancellor at the University of Nebraska in Omaha.

**Keith West**

West has set a record of firsts: first president of Mohave County Community College District, first superintendent of Mingus Union High School, and superintendent of Mohave Union High School District when the first high schools were built in Bullhead City and Lake Havasu City.

**Jack Whiteman**

Besides serving as President of the State Board of Education in 1980-81, Whiteman has contributed his time, talent, energy, and financial support to many education programs especially in the fine arts.

**Aura Mae Savage Williamson**

In the words of the present Yuma County Superintendent, Williamson stands out as an example of a teacher "who put her life into her work in the trenches for good or bad, for the long pull from college graduation to retirement here in Yuma County."

**Allen D. Yazzie**

In the early '60s, Yazzie was chair of the Navajo Education Committee and was instrumental in developing the Rough Rock Demonstration School and in encouraging Navajo leadership in education.

# The First Teachers' Strike

Lynn Meeks Jett

In the spring of 1971, which was my first year of teaching English at Scottsdale High School, salary negotiations broke down between the School Board and the Scottsdale Education Association. Heated exchanges took place, and we teachers attended School Board meetings and teacher solidarity meetings. Finally we had a huge teachers' meeting in the Scottsdale High School auditorium. People were talking about striking, but I thought "No way!". There had never been a teacher strike in Arizona, and I was convinced it was just a lot of show.

At the meeting, the SEA leaders said we should strike, The Scottsdale Federation of Teachers said they would support the strike, and suddenly we were being given a code of conduct for a strike—something we never got in our teacher preparation courses. We were to lock our desks and file cabinets, put everything away, leave no lesson plans, and be completely uncooperative so that anyone who came in to teach our classes would have a miserable time.

We were only out for three days, but it was one of the most awful experiences I've ever had. I was a first-year teacher, and I knew I was going to lose my job—that went without question. The options were to strike or to cross the picket line and be a scab knowing your buddies out there on strike were going to hate you forever. It was a very personal decision that each one of us had to make. Some, who didn't believe in strikes but who nevertheless supported their colleagues, solved the dilemma by calling in sick.

There must have been a day in between the meeting and the day we went out because I remember talking to my students about it. I told them that if the teachers went on strike, they would have to decide whether to come to school. If they did, I would not be there. In fact, I might not see them again because there was a good chance that I would be fired. The next morning I got up and drove to Scottsdale High School, and there we were, 90 percent of the faculty, on the picket line.

After fourteen years, what I remember most clearly was walking the picket line, back-and-forth, back-and-forth. We had shifts, and we had to keep moving or we would be loitering. And everytime I went around the circle, I would look into the faces of my friends. Although they weren't supposed to, some of the kids would come out and walk with us and put their arms around their teachers.

The worst time was when the School Board began busing in substitutes to keep the school open. Those on the picket line screamed out their frustration by being really vituperative.

What broke the strike was that after three days, the School Board got an injunction ordering everyone back in. When we met to discuss the injunction, we said, "Well, here we are. We're supposed to be role models for these children. If we don't go back into the classroom we're going to be breaking the law, and what kind of example is that to set?"

We were all worried about the students. A school strike isn't the same as turning off a machine and leaving a plant sitting idle. We were responsible for the kids. For many it was just a three-day holiday. Even those who came to school, weren't really being taught. In between his turns on the picket line, one of my friends held classes for his kids on the lawn of the nearby public library, but he was reprimanded for this by the administration.

Those of us on the strike had a common cause, and

we had rallys and our time on the line to build the kind of solidarity you hear about. But part of this solidarity was based on a resentment toward the people who would benefit equally if we made a good settlement but who would not take the risks we took. After the strike, things were never the same because it pitted teacher against teacher, teachers against the administration, and both teachers and administrators against the School Board. Principals, who really cared about their teachers, were in a terrible position because they had to obey the School Board and keep the schools open or lose their jobs immediately. After the settlement when everyone should have been working to heal the wounds, the administrators were ordered to write reports reprimanding us for participating. I believe they also docked our pay.

This furthered resentments between strikers and non-strikers. It wasn't as bad in my school which was 90 percent out as it was in those that were half-and-half. For at least five years after the strike, I remember going to in-service training sessions where the strikers sat together and the scabs sat together and there was almost visible hostility between the two. Leaders had to be careful in planning small-group activities because strikers refused to interact with non-strikers.

In one three-person physical education department, two out of the three had gone on strike. The two strikers would not speak to the scab. Finally it was so bad that one of the strikers was transferred to another school and a neutral third person was brought in to negotiate department decisions and keep the other two from vilifying one another in front of the students.

It seemed to me that after the strike there were lots of transfers and early retirements. The one woman in my department who had stayed had a good reason, I thought. Her husband was in law enforcement, and she felt that a strike was against the law and she could not break the law. But when we came back, people did not speak to her anymore. She soon moved on. It was through this kind of attrition, an actual change in the population of teachers, that the hostility was finally dissipated.

---

*Lynn Meeks Jett taught at Scottsdale High School until it was closed in 1982. She now teaches at Saguaro High in Scottsdale.*

---

## HIDING IN THE BUSHES

Wallace Myers

My wife, Bance Hom Myers, had a rather inauspicious beginning to her schooling. She is an ABC (American Born Chinese), and English was not spoken in her home. When she was five years old, her parents decided it was time for her to begin her formal education. On the first day of kindergarten, her father brought her to school, dropped her off, and left—no introductions, no filling out of forms, no farewell hug. For three consecutive days, Bance hid in the bushes until her father returned. On the fourth day, one of the other little girls found her and brought her into the classroom.

Once Bance got into school and learned English she did fine. She attended Arizona State University on a tennis scholarship, and today she is an internationally recognized chemical engineer.

*Wallace Myers is president of AmeriChem Engineering Services in Phoenix.*

---

# Six Years as a Traveling Poet

Alberto Rios

In 1968, the National Endowment for the Arts founded a Poets-in-the-Schools program, later changed to Writers-in-the-Schools, and finally to Artists-in-Education. Poets, authors, and artists go into schools not as teachers but as working professionals demonstrating what they do and letting children share in it. In the beginning years, most of our visits were for one or two weeks, but now schools are preferring longer periods, maybe a month, a semester, or a year.

The Arizona Commission on the Arts administers the program. I worked in it for six years, starting while I was still a graduate student in creative writing at the University of Arizona. Writers and artists who want to participate, submit a sample of their work to be screened by a panel of experts. The second step is an interview. For those accepted, a dossier is drawn up and sent out to the schools. The first year is mostly one of getting acquainted and watching other artists. Then a few invitations start to come in. If the visits go well, the word spreads and more invitations come. It's a matching fund arrangement with the school paying half the salary and the Arts Commission paying the other half.

We are not classroom teachers and do not necessarily have teaching certificates, so its against the law for the teacher to leave the room while one of us is there. I would start by talking with students about their ideas and feelings and then getting them to write. Sometimes I started with patterns or gimmicks, which creative kids very quickly went beyond. We read aloud and shared everyone's work. I would wait until almost the end to read my own poems because I didn't want to intimidate kids or give them a restricted idea of what I think poetry should be.

It was hard to tell when I was getting through to some kids, but every once in a while something would happen that would convince me I was succeeding. Once in Eloy a fire alarm went off and the kids were so involved in their writing that the teacher had to practically force them out of their seats. Another time in Florence, where I went several years in a row, I was starting my last-day sharing and I pulled out one of my books of poems and jokingly asked "Any requests?". A girl from the back row, who had sat sullenly all week, surprised me by raising her hand and saying, "Read that poem you read last year, that poem about your grandmother, the one you called 'Nani.'" I was amazed that she remembered me from a year ago, much less the specific poem and its title. It was about having troubles with Spanish and not being able to talk to my grandmother.

Once in Tucson, I had a hard time deciding whether I had succeeded or failed. I was in a junior high school where there were gangs—I mean real gangs that had real fights. One gang was called the "Young Classics," which I loved as a name, but feared as a group. Johnny, who was small in stature but big in hostility, was a member of this gang. He sat in the front row and everyday would come in and put his head on his desk with a big noise—whack! I knew I couldn't make him write, so for the first two or three days while I was getting the rest of the class involved in writing and sharing their efforts, I generally ignored him. But toward the end of the week when I had less talking to do to the class because they began doing more writing, I sat down with him asking such questions as why he didn't write, and what if someone wrote something about him, or what if he wrote something about someone else. His eyes sparkled at this idea, and he challenged me that if he wrote something would I read it to the class. I promised I would. He began writing about the other gang, mostly one obscenity after another. When he handed it to me, I read it aloud, just half saying the obscenities. The kids knew what was intended and there was much laughing and responding to the piece. Johnny beamed! He hadn't had that much attention all year.

The next day as soon as I arrived at the school, a girl came running up to ask if I had heard the news. Johnny had been beaten up. The other gang had done it to him because of the poem. I was horrified, and had this nagging feeling of fear and dread for myself as well as for Johnny. What had I done?

Sure enough, when he came to class a couple of hours later he had a black eye and bruises and scrapes, but much to my surprise he was radiant—a hero! He walked past me and with a sort of inconspicuous, thumbs-up gesture said, "It worked!" Then he sat down and started writing. He had learned the power of words.

To some kids, fighting is a medium of exchange, something they can understand while they can't understand just yet where poetry fits in. I was in a class made up mostly of cholos, boys who are today's version of pachucos. They wear black pants, black shiny shoes, two T-shirts (one for an undershirt and one for an outside shirt), and hairnets. I think the hairnets are a way of communicating that they are saving themselves for after school when the really important things begin to happen. I had been in this class several days and was sort of wrapping things up when a boy walked toward me with that tough cholo walk and his index finger pointed down, almost like a gun, "Hey, ese, you really like this poetry shit?"

He knew this wasn't appropriate talk for school. He was being dramatic and showing off, but he was genuinely curious and so I answered him, "Yeah, I do. It's my job."

"So, how many fights have you had?"

I don't think he was asking how tough I was, but rather how many fights it took for me to earn the freedom to be something so non-macho as a poet.

One of the things that I learned in going from school to school is how early children pick up cultural attitudes and stereotypes. I was in a Papago school outside of Sells working with a group of third and fifth graders. We walked to a pond quite a ways from the school because a lot of the kids had stories to tell about this pond. Coming back, the fifth graders all ran ahead and I was left behind with the third graders. I suggested we play a game to make the walk shorter, "Yeah, let's play cowboys and Indians!" someone shouted. Before the sentence was finished everyone was off and running calling out such things as "Run, run! The Indians are going to get you."

I was shocked, and after school talked with the principal about the incident. She told me to ask the children if they were Indians. The next day I started a conversation about cowboys and Indians, and in what was a grand learning moment for me found that these children do not think of themselves as Indians. They are Papago—actually O'odham because the tribe is changing its name to the old pronunciation. We talked about cowboy-and-Indian shows on television. These children could clearly see that they resemble the cowboys much more than the Indians. Television Indians are naked people wearing feathers and shouting war whoops while TV cowboys look like these children's fathers who drive pick-up trucks and wear western shirts, cowboy hats, Levis, and boots.

However, the children do not think of themselves as typical Anglo Americans either. The first day I was there I walked into a classroom before the bell had rung and heard a group chatting. I thought I understood what they were saying and so I joined in speaking Spanish. They understood me, but, in a surprised tone, asked "Where did you learn Papago?" They didn't realize that they were using so many Spanish words mixed in with their Papago that what they were speaking was almost as much my language as it was theirs.

In Glendale I had an experience with height that again showed how quickly kids pick up cultural attitudes and then struggle to make what they see fit into the system they have in their heads. I am 5'4" tall. The woman who was my liaison or hostess at this elementary school was close to 6' tall. She went with me for the first three days. Then on the fourth day she was ill and I went by myself. This little kid in the back of the room motioned for me to come over for a private conversation.

"Where's your wife?"

"That's not my wife."

"Oh, because she's taller than you?"

And then as if he just had a brilliant idea, he offered a solution to what he thought must be our problem, "High heels, huh?" He seemed so happy to have figured things out that I didn't disillusion him by pointing out that I would need something more like stilts than high heels, so I responded, "Yeah! That's right, I can get some high heels."

In the beginning phases of the artists-in-education program, regular classroom teachers were not always enthusiastic about us coming into their schools. They feared that a school board might attempt to save money by hiring one of us for a couple of weeks or a month rather than hiring an art or writing teacher for a whole year. But such fears have pretty much been dispelled because once parents come to see the advantages of giving their children experiences with the arts, they become supportive of having such experiences on a regular basis.

Of all the work I did in the program, I think my favorite was when Central Arizona College arranged for me to be a Poet-in-Residence for Pinal County. I have never heard of another county in the United States that had this kind of program. I did workshops in several communities and people could sign up for an hour's consultation on their own writing. We published a book of poems *Things Bigger Than We Are*. I worked in the project between 1980-82. I think it's still going on with different poets. It was a wonderful example of a school extending beyond the campus and beyond the typical school age group.

---

*Alberto Rios, a nationally known poet, grew up in Nogales, Arizona and is now on the creative writing faculty at ASU.*

---

## TEACHING AT AN INDEPENDENT SCHOOL

Dawn Lambson

After graduating from ASU in December of 1978, I spent the next few months substituting in different types of classrooms. The following summer I was looking for a permanent position and was contacted by LaNae Gore, who was opening her own New Horizons School for eighteen children between the ages of four and ten. She had already established a corporation, rented a building, and taken care of the legal qualifications. There were to be two teachers. I would teach lower form (kindergarten, first, and second grades).

By the end of August, we had prepared two classrooms and a learning lab which could be used either for group activities or for individual work and study. This lab was of particular importance to our philosophy of individualizing instruction. As school began and these eighteen unique children descended upon us, we found that meeting the needs of each one was both time consuming, and demanding. We spent hours evaluating the content and the context of text books and we built units from many texts and other materials.

We wanted the children to develop skills and gain knowledge, but we also wanted them to learn how to learn—to be able to take their understandings and abilities into every area of their lives. As part of this "education for living," we went on many field trips and involved children in challenging tasks.

Because of the time and energy expended, the first year was difficult but successful. We opened our second year with 31 students, three teachers, and the director. However because of finances, that was New Horizons' last year. The director had started the school not to make money but to provide quality education for her own children and those of other concerned parents. This made it especially sad to have to face the fact that such a small group of parents could not afford to maintain the kind of school we all wanted. At the end of the year, we began helping parents locate the best places for their children, many of whom went into gifted programs in the public schools.

*Dawn Lambson lives and teaches in Tempe.*

---

# A Regent Remembers

Rudy Campbell

One weekend in 1973 I was on a ladder out in the yard trimming a tree when my wife came out and said, "The Governor is on the phone and wants to talk to you." She must have told him I was up in a tree because when I picked up the phone, he started out with the Biblical reference, "Get thee down, Zacchaeus." We laughed and then he said, "Rudy, where did you go to school?" I didn't know he was asking a serious question and I said "Back east—I went to Mesa High School and that's east of Tempe, isn't it?" We laughed again, and then he went on to say "I just wanted to make sure that you hadn't graduated from the University of Arizona because I have appointed all the people I am going to appoint from the U. of A. to the Board of Regents. I am thinking of appointing you, Rudy. How would you feel about that?"

I was surprised and said, "Well, Governor, you ought to be careful of that because I didn't go to a university at all. You might be criticized for appointing someone who has no degree whatsoever." His response was, "Rudy, I want *business* people on the Board. Running the university at the Regents' level is primarily business—bond issues, funding, building, and so forth. The academic aspect of running the universities is taken care of by the administration."

I was tremendously honored, of course, and accepted the appointment. I had been the mayor of Tempe in 1968 and '69 and then served on the State Highway Commission for five years ending in 1973. When I was appointed to the Board of Regents, I was the first member ever to be appointed from Tempe. The majority of the Board has always been U. of A. alums. Dr. William Payne, who came after me, was the first ASU graduate to serve. But I did not come on the Board strictly as an advocate of ASU and Tempe. I came with the intention of being non-parochial. My experience as mayor had taught me that you can't serve just one district; you have to serve them all.

A member of the Board of Regents is appointed by the Governor for an eight-year term; today senate confirmation is necessary, but it didn't used to be. A regent can be removed only for cause. Every two years, two of the eight positions come up for appointment, except for the student regent who comes up every year. In addition to the eight members there is the Governor and the Superintendent of Public Instruction who are voting ex-officio members. This makes a total of ten voting members.

When Governor Williams appointed Ralph Bilby (who is now deceased) and myself in 1974, the entire Board was Williams appointees so we were all Republicans, which in my opinion was not really healthy. When Governor Castro was elected, he made all Democrat appointments.

One of the first things we had to deal with after I came on the Board was the open-meeting law. There were some members who did not like that law. They felt we could function better behind closed doors. It's true that in private we could argue things out and let our hair down and be more candid. But you simply can't do that anymore. I found that with all the reporters and other observers taking notes, I even had to be careful about asking a question because however I phrased my question was likely to be interpreted as my position on the issue. Having to be so careful was inhibiting.

The Board resisted the open-meeting law for a while after it was passed saying that it did not apply to us. But when Ralph Bilby and I came on the Board we thought that it did apply, and we convinced the other members that keeping the door closed caused more problems than it would to have the reporters because what people assumed we were saying was much worse than what was actually going on.

One particular long-time reporter from one of the radio stations was present at the first open-door meeting. He put his microphone right up in Elliott Dunseath's face because Elliott had been the most outspoken against having open meetings. Elliott handled it with good grace though and we got through that okay.

I was on the Board of Regents from 1974 to 1982. My term should have expired at the end of 1981, but we were in the midst of selecting a new president of the University of Arizona and the governor did not want to replace Dwight Patterson and me until that job was completed. We appointed all three of the current presidents while I was on the Board.

During my term, the students at the three Arizona universities successfully campaigned to have a student Regent. Initially I resisted the idea. What they originally asked for was three voting student regents, one from each school. That didn't fly. The voting thing was what really bothered me, as well as the number. Adding three members would make the Board too large and unwieldy to get anything done. When the students and the legislature finally simmered down to asking for one, non-voting student Regent, then I supported the idea. I thought it was good to have a student on the Board, but as I told students who discussed the issue with me, I had a college-age daughter and son and neither of them had the experience to start voting on matters of such consequence as those before the Regents. "It has nothing to do with how bright you are; it is just experience."

Once a young woman from one of the student newspapers was interviewing me. I said to her, "We're in the process right now of evaluating some outstanding bonds, about 13 million dollars worth. We're going to refund those for obvious reasons having to do with the current bond market. Now, are you familiar with that?"

"No, Mr. Campbell, I'm afraid I'm not," she replied. And I told her that neither were any of the other students because they just haven't had to deal with anything like that yet. Almost every one of us on the Board of Regents has had experience with a variety of similar issues and it would be unfair for students to be given votes on a type of problem they have never faced.

The way we set up the appointment of a student Regent was for each of the student government associations to select a candidate from which the governor makes the final choice. Each one comes on the Board with such enthusiasm; they're going to change the whole system! The first one from Tempe was Joel Steiner. Joel and I met for breakfast one morning soon after he was appointed. One of the big issues among the ASU students at that time was to have wine served in the Memorial Union. I told Joel I had been around long enough to know how you get things done. You start out taking things a little bit at a time. If we allow wine in the MU, then next year you're going to want beer because some of the students don't like wine. The year following that you're going to come back to ask for hard liquor. That's just the way it goes, I know! And I am opposed to that, I don't think there should be liquor of any kind on campus.

Co-ed dorms were pretty well on the way by then too, and there was no real opposition to that on my part. I did oppose, however, having birth control available at the health center. I didn't think we were obligated to offer that kind of service. I likened it to the liquor thing because I felt a vote of approval by the Board would indicate that we were condoning pre-marital sex. I explained to Joel that I didn't want a good mother from St. Johns, Arizona to have to worry about the kind of place she is sending her daughter. I think I have a responsibility to those people out there. They're expecting my conservative nature to be out front.

Joel said, "Mr. Campbell, I disagree with you, but I appreciate and respect you for telling me how you feel." There were other issues on which we disagreed, but Joel and I got along fine, as I did with all the other student Regents. They were outstanding kids who came from a variety of philosophical viewpoints just as did the rest of the Board members.

---

*Rudy Campbell, who lives in Tempe, shared these remembrances in an interview.*

# Four Generations in Arizona Schools

Mary Maffeo

Henry J. Maffeo was born in Ivrea, Italy on October 22, 1882. His parents brought him to Bisbee, Arizona as an infant, the second of five sons to be born to Joseph and Maria Maffeo. In 1977, when he was 95-years-old, he talked on tape about memories of his first schooling in 1889 on Brewery Gulch.

Henry's son, John H. Maffeo, was born in Globe, Arizona on April 19, 1914 in the same adobe house where his mother Ella Holohan Maffeo was born. He started to school in Phoenix at St. Mary's Grammar School in 1921. Sister Esperanza, who taught at St. Mary's for fifty-four years was his first teacher. John graduated from Phoenix Union High School in 1933. He played the lead in the Senior Class play *Seventh Heaven* under the direction of Mila Bray. He was head cheerleader with the Shortridge twins. But what turned the girl's heads was his 1929 Whippet roadster. He entered Phoenix College where he joined Tau Omega and learned to play bridge. He enrolled at Tempe Teacher's College where he learned he wasn't cut out for teaching, and left in 1935 to go into business with his father.

John Maffeo's daughter, Margaret Ella, who became "Mimi", was born in 1948, the second of seven children. She started school in Phoenix in 1954 at St. Francis Grammar School and spent 12 years there and at the adjacent campus of Xavier High School. In the early sixties she was active in the *Anytown* brotherhood organization and participated in a demonstration at the state capitol for a human rights commission for Arizona. Enrolled at Arizona State University in 1966, she joined a sorority and was chosen Pi Kappa Alpha "Dream Girl", but she also marched in anti-war demonstrations and worked for two well known professors, Dr. Herbert Stahnke, the "scorpion" expert, and Dr. Nick Salerno, who was ASU's first TV personality, showing movies on Channel 8, KAET.

Mimi Maffeo married Jim Cordalis after graduation in 1970. Their son Kelly was born in 1975. Unlike his mother, grandfather, and great grandfather, who all started school at six or seven, Kelly was enrolled at Palo Alto preschool at four. The rising tide of inflation and the goals of the women's movement made early schooling a common occurrence. Kelly "graduated" from preschool to Bustos Elementary, where his first teachers nurtured his interest in reading and writing. Lydia Casillas and Gene Steer taught skills that made a second-grade school newspaper an exciting event and journalism a possible career choice. When Kelly graduates from eighth grade in 1989, it will mark 100 years of education for the Maffeo family in Arizona, and the beginning of a second century of progress. A statement from each of these four follows.

*Henry J. Maffeo (from a tape made in 1977):* My first school teacher was Belle Granville. She and her sister Phoebe were the best looking girls you ever saw in your life, well-proportioned too and smart. The mother was a great big woman. The father did the assessment work for the Shattuck mine. Oh God damn, he was the funniest built feller, just as wide as he was long. He used to ride an old sorrell horse. Anyway, Belle was my teacher. When my father died I was just a little feller, seven-years-old. I didn't know I wasn't supposed to go to school the day my father died, so I went. Belle Granville took me aside and explained it to me, and I understood what she was talking about, so I went on home."

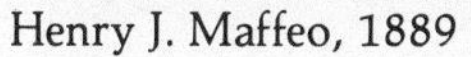

Henry J. Maffeo, 1889

John Maffeo, 1932

Mimi and Kelly Cordalis, 1984

*John Maffeo:* I always wanted to eat at the PUHS cafeteria because that was where all the other kids ate, but my parents said "No, you live close enough to school that you can come home for lunch." Sometimes I would go over to Grosso's cafe on 4th Street and get a big plate of potatoes and brown gravy for 15 cents. Nothing has ever tasted that good since.

Not everything during the depression was as grim as people make it sound. For example, anyone who went to Phoenix Union in the 1930s remembers the Masque of the Yellow Moon. This pageant began in the 1920s and continued on into the mid '50s. When I was participating, it was just students from Phoenix College and Phoenix Union, but later all the high schools joined in. Art teacher Cordelia Perkins created the scripts and directed the Masque while Margaret Hurley was in charge of the final dance number. The Masque was held in late April or early May. Once it was over, school just limped along until the end. Each year we had different themes, usually something about Arizona or southwest history. The backdrops were huge creations which turned the football field into a stage. Over 2,000 students participated, helped out by wagons, horses, waterfalls, or whatever Mrs. Perkins thought up. We practiced so much that everything was supposed to go like clock-work, but some little thing always went wrong. One year the band stopped playing before the dancers were finished and Laurette Briniger made a mad dash over to tell Mr. Etzweiler to start up again. My senior year, Juhn McCalla was the queen. In 1983, when she came to our fifty-year class reunion, I still thought of her as queen of the Masque.

*Mimi Maffeo Cordalis:* I was a third grader at St. Francis Elementary in Phoenix in 1956. One of our favorite games on the playground was to come up behind someone, put our hands over their eyes, and call out "guess who?". I was usually adept at guessing, but one particular day I was stumped. Teresa? Nancy? I rattled off the names of all conceivable possibilities. Who was left? I give. Turning around, shocked at the revelation, I saw Sister Mary Damaris.

She was a teacher and one that I idolized. It was the first time I realized that teachers were people. They had lives, played games, and had fun. Today, I am a teacher at Frye Elementary in Chandler. As I look around at my class of fifth graders, I wonder how many of them think my life begins as I walk in the door and ends as they exit.

*Kelly Cordalis (taken from a journal kept at Crismon School in Mesa where Kelly was a third grader in 1983-84):* My faverite subject is spelling. That's not only my favrite subject it's also my best subject. I don't know why but I've alwese been good at spelling, my dad is a bad speller but for some reson I'm a good speller. My mom's pretty good but I'm better.

---

*Mary Maffeo works for the Dougherty Scholarship Foundation which has ties back to territorial days and the estate left by M. J. G. Dougherty.*

# Glimpses: 1960-1985

## MOVING INTO THE COMPUTER AGE
## Bette Priest

While I was working on my Master's degree in Elementary Education at ASU, Dr. Gary Bitter teased me into taking some computer classes. I kept saying "I am not good at math, I am a third grade teacher—we *only* get into multiplication!" He persisted, and in 1981 I took a computer literacy course. Our class unpacked and set up the thirty brand new Apple III's for the College of Education micro computer lab. That fall, I took the BASIC programming class from Dr. Gerlach. There was so much homework to do that I decided if I were to see my family we had to get a computer at home. We purchased a basic system—the monitor, keyboard, one disc drive, and a printer. I took more computer classes and found I enjoyed them. Quite a change in attitude! Last winter when the Tempe district provided six computers for my school, another teacher and I started an after school course for the faculty, explaining definitions and parts and teaching elementary programming as an aid to the evaluation of software.

In the last two years, I have also taught BASIC to kids in summer school, grades four through nine. There was a ten-minute break between the second and third hours and since that was the only time I could go to the bathroom, I didn't allow the kids to come in the room until the bell rang. However the seventh- through ninth-graders didn't always listen. Once when I came back, a couple of the boys were scuffling. I broke it up and asked what was going on. They had both wanted to get on the same computer. I said "OK, you're both off for 20 minutes. You can listen to the discussion, and then if you behave and shake hands, you can come back on." They acted as though I had sentenced them to *die*. "Please, Mrs. Priest, we won't do it anymore! Make it five minutes, please? We're shaking hands now, see?" I said "*No*, 20 minutes."

After the 20 minutes were up, the two of them walked to an empty machine, and happily worked together for the rest of the class. Even when three students had to work on one terminal there were seldom any problems because they did not want to waste the groups' computer time. They were learning cooperation and group interaction along with computer skills.

Down the line, I think schools will have a terminal at each desk. Some districts are waiting to see if it doesn't all blow over, but barring a nuclear disaster, computers are not going to go away. There will always be paper and pencil and books, but also computers because they will allow teachers to individualize instruction so that slower children will be able to work at their own pace, and faster children won't be tied to a particular text book or the overall class rate of progress. The trade-offs of computer-assisted instruction will enhance the teaching of skills and in the end provide a better education for kids.

*Bette Priest, on a year's leave of absence from Nevitt School, is working on a Master's degree in Educational Technology at ASU.*

## 25 YEARS OF CHANGE
## Robert L. Stevens

In 1956 when I came out to what is now Northern Arizona University as a young English instructor, I had several Indians in my classes. Having spent most of my life in Illinois, I didn't think of them as Navajos, Hopis, or Apaches. They were all just Indians and all distinguished by speaking, reading, and writing English as if it were a foreign language—as, indeed, to them it was. Though I had no background in teaching English as a second language, I knew that they needed help and I tried to do what I could.

One alert young man I remember especially well. I believed that his most urgent problem was an inability to read the fairly difficult freshman English reader adopted for the class, and I decided to help him with some of the articles. I knew that we needed a simpler text to start with, but I decided that a familiarity with these articles would at least allow him to take part in class discussion. In the drill, I simply helped him read an article aloud and then discussed with him each paragraph as he completed it.

As I said, he was an alert young man, and he once stopped in the middle of a sentence to ask the meaning of the phrase *Dresden china*. This question showed that he was trying to grasp what he read, and I launched into a discussion of the kind of china that had been manufactured in Dresden since the 18th century. I was starting to tell him about Dresden's virtual destruction in World War II, when he interrupted me. "No," he said, "What is china?" It was my first realization of the cultural gulf that separated us and of the problems facing all those young people who sought an education as strangers in a land grown strange before their eyes.

Their children are coming to college now, but what a difference! Now without looking up from my desk I cannot tell a Navajo or Hopi youth from an Anglo. Many come from homes in which English is the dominant language and they speak it as their first language. Somewhere along the line a choice was made or certain inevitabilities began to assert themselves, and, following the example of the Italians, Germans, Swedes, Norwegians, Chinese, Japanese, and others before them, they are now immigrating to America.

With the embracing of the Anglo culture comes the concomitant letting go of the native culture. Scholars are at work today studying and perserving knowledge of the native languages that are in danger of being lost. Ekkehart Malotki, of NAU, for instance, has said that the Hopi language is fading away with the passing of each generation. Malotki is working to preserve the Hopi language and culture by transposing what has heretofore been oral tradition into the written word, thereby saving it for future generations.

In the mere quarter of a century since I came to NAU a momentous change has taken place. Today, I would not have to define *china—Dresden*, maybe, but not *china*.

*Robert L. Stevens is Professor Emeritus of English at Northern Arizona University in Flagstaff where he lives.*

## WESTWOOD HIGH SCHOOL—A GOOD BEGINNING
### Fern B. Yerby

When Westwood High School in Mesa opened in 1963, we had no gymnasium, no auditorium, and no special equipment. Even so, we had memorable programs and pep rallies staged on a make-shift platform out-of-doors overlooking the athletic field. Morale was high. Under the coaching of Edgar "Mutt" Ford, the Warriors football team was undefeated. The City Council and business and professional clubs in Mesa supported the school by sponsoring student organizations, furnishing qualified and experienced speakers, and giving awards to outstanding students. These incentives helped everyone excel.

I taught in the business department, and in the beginning we had no typewriters. For six weeks we taught typing techniques and the keyboard on "picture" keyboards placed on each typing desk. It worked surprisingly well—no frustration from typing errors! When the IBM Selectrics arrived, the transition was simple and exciting.

Our advanced typing course included units covering the resumé, the job interview, proper office dress and etiquette, filing, duplicating, etc. Many of the students enrolling were not ready for these tasks because they were only in the eighth or ninth grade when they had their first year of typing. We formed a trial intermediate typing class, and at the end of the school year the State Department of Education evaluated the course positively and Intermediate Typing became a permanent course at Westwood as well as at most other high schools in Arizona.

For a while, *Opportunity Hall* was located in portable classrooms on our campus. This was a special school for students troubled with drugs and other problems. Our principal was interested in the welfare, safety, and morale of all students. However, the image of our school suffered, and we were all happy when it was possible for these students to have a campus of their own.

In 1984, Westwood was judged one of the nation's outstanding schools. This made me think back to its beginning under a remarkable principal, Elias R. Brimhall. Teachers and students stepped softly in his presence because he was firm and had high standards. But we teachers could teach with confidence knowing that if we were doing a good job he would stand behind us.

*Fern B. Yerby taught at Westwood High School from 1963 until she retired in 1976. She now lives in Mesa.*

## A CLASS VISIT TO VESTA BREAD, MARICOPA POTTER
### Mitzi Schireman

In 1969 one of my students gave me a small piece of Indian pottery which was painted a rusty red and decorated with a black design. Almost round, about the size of a tangerine, it had a small one inch hole in the top, just large enough to slip in a few dried flowers. It had been made by my student's grandmother, Vesta Bread, a Maricopa Indian.

Later in the school year, I visited Mrs. Bread on the Gila River Reservation and made arrangements for my Southwest Literature class to visit her and watch her make pottery. On that first visit my students from Tolleson Union High School gathered around a table Mrs. Bread had set up in her yard. After a few questions, the students soon became involved in her work.

"Where does the clay come from?" asked one of the students.

Her answer was a simple one. "I dig it myself somewhere away from here."

Mrs. Bread started her vase from a slightly concave circle of clay onto which she gradually added coils. As she smoothed these coils out with her fingers or a broken piece of pottery and water, the tall vase began to take shape.

I had asked Mrs. Bread to show pottery in different stages of preparation so the students could see the whole process. When the vase was nearly finished, she stopped and explained the other steps in her pottery making.

She took a small piece of cloth and dipped it into a bowl of liquid red clay and painted another small bowl which was already dry. She told the students this red clay came from the Superstition Mountains.

I was as fascinated as the students because I realized that what we were seeing was a dying art. Mrs. Bread was one of the last of the old Maricopa potters.

After the bowl was painted, it was set aside to dry. The next step, explained Mrs. Bread, was to polish the dry red bowl using special stones from the river bottom. These were small flat rocks which she had used for a long time, and which fit perfectly into her hand. I tried to polish the red bowl using one of the stones. It wasn't as easy as it looked to get the shiny, rust color associated with the Maricopa style.

The firing process was a simple one. The polished pottery was set on wire over hot mesquite coals and covered with sheets of old tin roofing. When the fire died out and the pottery cooled, it was removed.

The final step that Mrs. Bread showed my students was the adding of the black designs. The black liquid was made by boiling mesquite bark and small twigs. She used a piece of wood almost like a toothpick except that the tip which she dipped in the juice to paint the designs with was rather soft. What fascinated all of us was that she drew the designs free-hand. On the round bowl the one end of the design met the other end, and when it was finished we could not tell where she had begun. All kinds of simple geometric designs decorated other pieces of pottery sitting on the table.

When Mrs. Bread was finished and it was time for us to leave, I had made arrangements for her to give each of the students one of the little pieces of pottery like the one I had first been given. I later purchased some of Mrs. Bread's pottery for myself. At first she did not sign her work, but I asked her to sign my pieces. It was thrilling when I later visited the Heard Museum and the Northern Arizona Museum and found Maricopa pottery signed by Vesta Bread.

Before her death in 1976, I took other classes to visit Mrs. Bread, and I wish now that we could have videotaped one of those visits. But even without a videotape, I will always remember that first visit. Because of its impact on me, I wrote this poem:

**The Maricopa Potter**

There she sits, the ancient one,
Leather-lined face framed by a ragged red scarf,
The past returns and the white man's world
  fades into oblivion as the knotted brown fingers
  pat, pat, pat the mound of clay into shape.

"What are you making, Grandmother?"
"A pot, a wedding pot."
"Who takes a wife, Old One?"
"My grandson . . ."

The voice fades into an almost forgotten prayer—
"Spirit of the Clay, make this vessel into
  one of beauty and honor,
Let the power of my hands mold it
  into a pitcher of strength."

The shape is finished, and age-tired bronze
  matriarch
  nods in the warming sun
  as Halos dries her gift of love.

*Mitzi Schireman has taught and worked in the Tolleson Union High School for 22 years.*

## WHAT 57 SCHOOL BUSES CAN DO
## John Goss

The last week of September in 1983, southern Arizona experienced record rainfall. On Saturday October 1, flooding began all along the rivers of southern Arizona, especially the Santa Cruz. I am the director of physical facilities and transportation for the Marana School District, which stretches over 550 square miles. Several of our 57 buses were out that afternoon transporting students to athletic and other extra-curricular events. What in the morning had been a slightly muddy desert was by late afternoon a criss-cross of running washes and impassable rivers. I live in Tucson and was on the radio with the bus drivers and the sheriff's office trying to set up alternate routes to get the kids back to their respective schools and homes. As evening came on, the sheriff's office directed us to give up on getting the students home. We were to get them off the roads and into an evacuation center set up at Estes School in Marana where the local police and fire department had already been taking people all afternoon.

I went to the school as fast as I could arriving there about 11:00 that night. By then, it was obvious that everyone had to move from this location as the water was already on the playground. School buses and trucks from the National Guard were used to transport these 500 people approximately 11 miles to the Thornydale school which is on higher ground.

West of the Santa Cruz River in the Avra Valley, people were completely cut off. The assistant superintendent, several bus drivers and some cafeteria workers who lived nearby, along with the local fire department, organized and ran an evacuation center in the gymnasium of Marana High School. Even the Red Cross couldn't get in. Food was provided from that stored in the cafeteria. Several hundred people spent Saturday through Monday there. When I arrived late Monday afternoon, I was welcomed as the first "outsider" to get through.

Communication was a major problem. All telephones and electricity were out. Police radios have to be recharged, and since there was no electricity with which to recharge them we ended up relying on the radios in the school buses. Fortunately for us, our buses were already spread throughout the valley because most of the drivers park them in their own yards at night. I used every method except carrier pigeons to contact the bus drivers and get them to take their buses where they were needed. Because the radios couldn't transmit over the Tucson Mountains, we relayed messages through a dispatch center. It was slow but terribly important in helping family members locate each other. We had a bus parked outside of each center just to transmit messages.

After the waters began to recede, we wanted to start school, and so we began moving people out of the High School and Thornydale and back into Estes School where there was extra space. Again, National Guard trucks and school buses were used. Some evacuees stayed in the Estes School for ten days, but the Red Cross rather than school personnel did the management.

In most classrooms, the water had been only four-to-six inches deep, and our school maintenance people worked around the clock using fire hoses to wash out the mud. Students were back in their classes by Wednesday morning. Of course we lost a few books and things from the lower shelves, but in general we were fortunate. The only major repair was the auditorium in the junior high. It had a sloping floor, and the water rose to a foot over the stage. When we started doing the repairs we decided to do some remodeling at the same time. During the process, we found asbestos, which we decided to have removed. It was the winter of 1985 before we got back into the auditorium.

But the longest lasting effect of the flood is probably mental rather than physical. It is in people's attitude. There is a new feeling of confidence that when there's an emergency, we can all work together: schools, law enforcement agencies, the Red Cross, the National Guard, and townspeople. It was inspiring to see that 500 people could live peacefully for three days in a school gymnasium and classrooms without even having cots to sleep on.

*John Goss gave this report in a telephone interview.*

## COLLEGE VIA TELEVISION
## Velma S. Cooper

In the summer of 1948 when I was sixteen years old, I married John Cooper, my childhood sweetheart. That fall, he attended his second year at Arizona State College while I finished my last year of high school at Tempe Union, one of the few schools in the valley that would allow married girls to attend. We lived in Victory Village, government subsidized trailers for returning veterans located where Grady Gammage Auditorium now stands. After graduation, we returned to the family cattle ranch at Wagoner which has been in the Cooper family for over seventy-five years.

I spent about five years riding the range with my husband before we had children. When I discovered that a course in Basic Russian was offered on television, I enrolled, sending back east for the books. When September came, I learned that Phoenix Evening College offered television classes for credit. My husband, in Phoenix for supplies, registered me. Dean Mildred Bulpitt was very helpful. When I continued to take everything offered, she realized I had acquired almost enough credits to graduate, and she arranged specific courses so that I would be eligible for a degree. I graduated with the Evening College, but continued taking more courses.

In September of 1965, my husband, reading the newspaper, mentioned that ASU was registering for the fall semester. "Why don't you go down and get your teacher's certificate?" John and I, aware that cattle ranching alone would not continue to support the family, had decided to start a children's ranch to supplement our income. A teacher would make the project more reliable. I didn't answer him, but later got to thinking about it and went out on the hill where he was welding and asked if he really meant it. His answer was, "Yes."

When he came in that evening, he was surprised to see I had everything packed. He took the children and me to Phoenix the next day. I finagled my transcript from Phoenix College and enrolled at ASU as an elementary education major. A year later, I encouraged my husband to also come to town and get his teaching certificate. Two years later, aware that not even a children's ranch would be as profitable as teaching in the public schools, I applied to Alhambra school district, and was hired. I have taught fifth grade at Barcelona for the past seventeen years while my husband has taught in Washington School District for sixteen years. Thanks to my husband's persistence and to television classes, the ranch is still in our name.

*The Alhambra and Washington school districts are in Phoenix where the Coopers live.*

## READING IS FUNDAMENTAL
**Barbara Ronan**

In the late 1960s, I lived next door to a wonderful minister, Reverend Ralph Supplee, who was involved in more good causes than one man could handle. He was always looking for help, and one day he came over to tell me that being the mother of five children wasn't enough of a challenge for me. Surely I would want to help with a new program called Reading is Fundamental. This program, which is supported by volunteers and donations from businesses and individuals, has as its goal helping kids learn to love reading by letting them select books to keep for their own.

One of the things that educators have discovered about children who do well in school is that most of them have books in their homes and parents who enjoy sharing these books with their children. The Reading is Fundamental program tries to make this condition a possibility for all children, not just a privileged few. I couldn't argue with the soundness of the idea or the value of the project. And then Reverend Supplee assured me that this noble cause would not take more than two or three hours a week.

He must have known this was an understatement, but I doubt that he had any idea of how the Reading is Fundamental program would change my life. It became a full-time job, and to my surprise I soon found myself at airports trying to convince the authorities not to make me pay excess baggage fees when I was flying with eighteen boxes of books to Winslow or Nogales. I was even more surprised to find myself driving a book mobile across lonely deserts, through mountain passes, and alongside canyon cliffs while getting to Tonalea, Oraibi, Polacca, Keams Canyon, Greasewood, Ganado, Ft. Defiance, Window Rock, Canyon de Chelly, or Kayenta. We had an 800 mile route covering both the Hopi and Navajo Reservations that we would take two or three times a year.

But we did not go just to the Indian Reservations. We took books anyplace where we thought children needed them and where the local community would lend support. At one inner city school in Phoenix, the principal was convinced that we would increase littering rather than literacy. He was sure that the children would be happy to participate in the free distribution, but from previous experience in trying to send things home, he was equally sure that many of the books would be tossed aside. He had a clean-up crew all ready. The next day when he called to tell us that he was wrong—not a single book was found on the school grounds—he was as happy as we were.

It's always a thrill to see children choose books, but I guess my favorite memories come from the Indian Reservations because there the books seemed to be so much more appreciated. Parents and teachers frequently said they wished there had been such a program when they were young. One teacher told me that in her home there had been absolutely no reading material and that she was in the sixth grade before she read a book.

As much as I loved the children, my favorite memory is of an adult man. He looked to be about sixty-years-old. I noticed him standing outside the book van watching with intense interest as the children entered and then came out with their books. This was up on Second Mesa on the Hopi Reservation. I went outside and told the man a little about the program and said that if he wanted to he would be welcome to come in and select a book for himself. I was busy with the children, but I was aware that he examined many

books before he selected one. Finally, he came and showed me what he had chosen. It was Robert Louis Stevenson's *Treasure Island*. As he said thank you, he explained that he knew the book already. He remembered it from when he went to boarding school in California. For some reason he had not finished the book, but "Now," he said, "I can find how it turned out!"

*Barbara Ronan, who lives in Scottsdale, was the Western Regional Director of Reading Is Fundamental from 1969-76.*

## WAS COLLEGE EVER THUS?
### Leonard Ingraham

As a lifetime resident of New York City I began working in the public schools in the early 1930s eventually becoming city-wide director of social studies. When it was time to retire at age 60, I began looking around to find what else I could do. In the spring of 1973 I came to Tempe to be interviewed for an ASU College of Education position in teaching methods of social studies. Palm trees, oranges hanging undisturbed, graffiti-free walls and sidewalks, and young people with spirit and decorum made the few days I spent in Tempe a study in contrasts between my future and my past. The sharpest contrast was between the calm and friendly interview that included a party at a faculty member's home and the numerous hurdles presented in moving up the civil service career-ladder of the New York City schools where written tests, teaching tests, performance records, observations, and high pressure were the order of the day.

I spent ten of the most pleasant, enjoyable, and stimulating years of a fifty-year career teaching at ASU, then came compulsory retirement because of age. It was time for a new career. My wife has always said, "I married you for better or worse but not for lunch," and my physician advises keeping occupied. So when Ottawa University called and offered me an adjunct faculty contract from August 1983 to November 1983 to teach "An Introduction to Curriculum" for four undergraduate credits to a single student in my home, I signed a contract. Ottawa University is not located in Canada, but in Kansas, and since 1977 has had a non-residential center in Phoenix. A conference was held to plan the course of study with one of the three permanent staff members and the student. Then she met with me at my home for six sessions of one-and-a-half hours each, completed her assignments, and passed a take-home final examination. She was to graduate in May of 1984 and take a position at a community college where she would teach students interested in her field, that of a respiratory technician.

At the end of 1983, a former colleague recommended me to Nova University, a Fort Lauderdale institution which offers graduate "education modules" in 12 cities in Florida, and in Las Vegas and Phoenix. "Modern Curriculum Design" was to be given for three credits on four successive Saturdays, six hours per day. I arranged to team-teach since six hours a day was too much for this retiree. The class members came from a variety of ethnic backgrounds; they were attentive, cooperative, and most of all productive. During the four weeks, two of the men became new fathers. The mother of one of the infants was also a student and at the third session brought the ten-day-old child with her. She nursed him at the back of the room where he slept quietly the rest of the day—the youngest attendee in my fifty years of teaching. All students received passing grades, and the newborns were each presented with a gold star.

The whole experience was a far cry from City College of New York, class of 1933, but then this was 1984 and who knows what lies ahead?

*Professor Emeritus from ASU, Leonard Ingraham lives in Scottsdale.*

## WHAT I DID LAST SUMMER
### Kami Merrill

Editor's Note: *Today, school field trips have become international with hundreds of Arizona high school students spending between two-weeks and a year in foreign countries arranged through service organizations or privately sponsored tours for language students. We asked one of these students, fourteen-year-old Kami Merrill of Tempe, to write about her experience in being host to a German house guest for a month and then returning the visit by spending June, 1984 with his family in Grenvach-Wyhlen.*

I don't think I've ever been so excited as the night the Germans came. My friends did their best to calm me down, but really there was nothing they could have done. In some situations (such as this one) my hyperactivity is uncontrollable. The exchange student who was going to live with my family came off the plane last. He looked much nicer in person than in the picture we were sent. After a month of parties and excursions to various statewide scenic sites, the German invasion ended, and we all found ourselves beginning homework and catching up on those things we had somehow avoided—including friends, who by this time were fairly ticked off.

Without the visitors, life seemed incredibly dull, but we German students began counting one month, two days, five hours, and thirty-six minutes until we would board a plane for Frankfurt. The day finally came and I have never been so scared. I tried to focus my thoughts on the trip though and the fun I would experience. No tears ruined my mascara as I said my final *aus weder sehen*. Somehow I was going to be tough, real tough even though I was the youngest one in the group.

I started studying German when I was in seventh grade. I don't remember how I got interested, but my mother says it was because a cute German exchange student stayed with our neighbors for a month. After he left I began badgering her to get me a tutor. She held off thinking it was a passing fancy, but I persisted and she finally found a university student to come and instruct me. Then when I was getting ready for eighth grade, we found out that first-year German in nearby McClintock High School was taught the first hour. By getting up an hour early, I could go to German class and then on to my own junior high. I didn't like the high school kids yelling "Oh, look, the eighth grader is here!" but it was pretty funny when I got the highest grade in the class.

This year I'm the only freshman in a second-year German class. My teacher suggested I move to third-year German, but I said no. I also declined the chance to apply for a year-long stay in Germany; there are some things I'm just too young for.

## THEY'RE STILL DOING ARITHMETIC AT WICKENBURG'S OLD GARCIA SCHOOLHOUSE
### Jeanne Marie Scott

Because the population waxed and waned with the fortunes of the Vulture Mine, there was no school in the Wickenburg Mining District until 1879. After several tentative beginnings, in 1884 a schoolroom was officially established in Wickenburg down by the Hassayampa in an adobe building owned by Ed Grant, a school trustee with a growing family. Trustee Fritz Brill also had school-age children but brought public schooling to a halt halfway through the 1885 year by marrying the teacher, Laura Copeland.

With the coming of the Phoenix and Prescott Railroad in 1895, the need for more space was met by bringing an 1880's wooden building over from the Vulture Mine and placing it on land owned by Don Ignacio Garcia, a Trustee and the man considered the "father" of Wickenburg education. Schoolmates Ann Wisdom (Purdy) and Lee Roberts, both now in their nineties, remember the decrepit old whitewashed schoolhouse, with the cold wind and the insects coming up through the gaps in the floorboards. They hated the job of going to the nearest well for the daily bucket of fresh water which stood, with its dipper, in the opposite corner from the wood-burning stove.

By 1905 a red-brick schoolhouse had replaced the wooden one on the 200-foot square opposite the Catholic church. On the same lot was the circa 1909 brick town jail. The older boys would boost each other up to look into the cells. When caught by the constable, they

# COMMUNITY BANK

## GARCIA SCHOOL OFFICE

got a whole new type of education by being given a "tour" of the jail.

In 1908, the one-room schoolhouse became graded when it was divided into two rooms. Other changes followed rapidly: in 1920, a second building was added on the site. In 1928, a new high school was built elsewhere. The number of students and buildings increased dramatically over the war years, and in the late fifties the buildings on the original Garcia site became the middle school. The 1905 red brick schoolhouse was remodelled as a library with acoustical tile walls and ceiling. School enrollment continued to grow and the once-quiet corner became a center of downtown traffic. Following a 1978 fire which destroyed the largest of the middle-school buildings, a decision was made to move the middle school out to West Wickenburg.

Since 1981, the school district, the town government, and private developers have been working on an adaptive use for the old Garcia schoolhouse, which is on the National Historical Register. Today, it has become the Community Bank, restored as closely as possible to the original wooden ceiling and sanded floor-board interior. There are some improvements since 1905 including running water in the basement. For lighting, "schoolhouse" electric globes hang from the ceiling instead of oil-filled wall lamps. The portraits of George and Martha Washington on either side of the forty-five star flag are by Currier and Ives. Hanging from the new picture rail are Smithsonian Museum copies of prints depicting President Theodore Roosevelt and his vice-President Charles Fairbanks. A wall museum of school memorabilia is slowly accumulating above the oak desks of bank manager Dale Joyce and his staff. Bank President Gary Johnson plans school yard landscaping to surround the newly refurbished exterior.

The playground swings arrive this month, January 1985.

*Jeanne Marie Scott, Wickenburg's town historian, is writing a booklet on the Garcia School and other territorial schools in Maricopa County. She would appreciate receiving information on Districts #2 through #8.*

# Index of Arizona People and Schools